Science Foundations

Chemistry

Bryan Milner and Ray Oliver

CAMBRIDGE
UNIVERSITY PRESS

Series Editor	Bryan Milner
Chemistry Editor	Ray Oliver
Authors	Peter Evans
	Helen Norris
	Ray Oliver
Consultants	Nigel Heslop
	Martyn Keeley
	Helen Norris

PUBLISHED BY THE PRESS SYNDICATE OF THE UNIVERSITY OF CAMBRIDGE
The Pitt Building, Trumpington Street, Cambridge, United Kingdom

CAMBRIDGE UNIVERSITY PRESS
The Edinburgh Building, Cambridge CB2 2RU, UK
40 West 20th Street, New York, NY 10011–4211, USA
10 Stamford Road, Oakleigh, VIC 3166, Australia
Ruiz de Alarcón 13, 28014 Madrid, Spain
Dock House, The Waterfront, Cape Town 8001, South Africa

http://www.cambridge.org

© Cambridge University Press 1997

First published 1997
Reprinted 1997, 1998, 1999, 2001 (twice)

Printed in the United Kingdom at the University Press, Cambridge

Typeset Stone Informal 10/13.5 pt

A catalogue record for this book is available from the British Library

ISBN 0 521 55663 5 paperback

Designed and produced by Gecko Limited, Bicester, Oxon
Cover photo: Laboratory glassware, Images Colour Library

Contents

Structure and bonding

Patterns of chemical change

Handling data   172

Revising for tests and examinations   175

What you need to remember: completed passages   176

Glossary/index   187

▦ Acknowledgements

6, 7, 8cr, bl, bc, 9t, ct, bl, br, 10c, b, 11, 16b, 17, 21, 22, 38, 42, 44, 45, 46cl, c, cr, b, 47, 55, 58, 59, 61, 71r, 72, 80, 94, 97c, b, 99, 104, 106, 107, 108, 109, 112c, b, 115, 118, 119, 134r, 138, 141c, r, 142, 147bl, br, 148, 150 (except t), 151b, 153, 154, 159l, Andrew Lambert; 8tr, 16ct, 71l, Werner Reith/Photo Images; 8br, 46tr, Malcolm Fife; 9cb, A S Gould; 10tr, TRH Pictures/Boeing; 16t, Richard Sewell, RKS Photography; 16cb, TRH Picture/MoD; 23, D Dennis; 24, The Natural History Museum, London; 30, Kathie Atkinson/Oxford Scientific Films; 37, 81b, 93, 131, 147t, Graham Portlock/Pentaprism; 35tl, Jim Winkley/Ecoscene; 35tr, Susan Cunningham/Panos Pictures; 35bl, 86b, Erik Schaffer/Ecoscene; 35br, Bridget Hodgkinson/Ecoscene; 41, Ian Robertson; 49, Ben Osborne/Oxford Scientific Films; 50, courtesy of British Cement Association; 52t, Hjalmar R Bardarson/Oxford Scientific Films; 52b, 53tr, b, GeoScience Features Library; 53tl, Science Photo Library; 81t, 134c, Michael Brooke; 86t, Adrian Davies/Bruce Coleman Ltd; 97tl, tr, Dave Carter Photography; 112t, TRH Pictures/US Navy; 128, Martyn F Chillmaid/Oxford Scientific Films; 132, courtesy of Manchester City Engineers; 134l, Chinth Gryniewicz/Ecoscene; 141l, 156, 157, 159r, Nigel Cattlin/Holt Studios International; 150t, The Kobal Collection/©1982 Paramount Pictures Corp.; 151t, 152, Biophoto Associates; 158, Mary Evans Picture Library

What's special about metals?

We use metals for lots of different things. Our lives wouldn't be the same without them.

1 Write down the names of all the metals in the pictures.

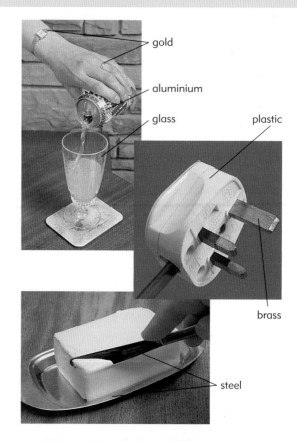

How can we tell which materials are metals?

Gold, copper, aluminium and steel are all called metals because they are like each other in some ways. We say that they have the same properties.

2 Write down two ways in which the metals in the pictures are like each other.

It is not always easy to tell whether something is a metal or not. We have to look at lots of its properties.

Can we know something is a metal just by looking?

Gold is always bright and shiny but most metals seem dull on the surface. If we scratch or cut a metal, the new surface is **shiny**. It becomes dull because the metal reacts with oxygen from the air to make a dull coat. Substances that are not metals are usually not shiny, even when you cut them.

3 Is the bar in the photograph made of metal? Give a reason for your answer.

Metals let heat and electricity pass through them

Both **heat** and **electricity** flow easily through all metals. We say that metals are good conductors of heat and electricity. This is a good way to tell the difference between metals and non-metals. If we know that a substance conducts electricity, then we are almost sure that it is a metal. The only non-metal that conducts electricity well is a type of carbon called graphite.

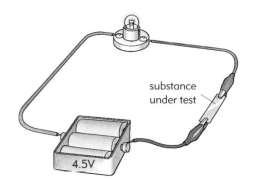

substance under test

4.5V

4 Is the substance in the diagram a metal? Give a reason for your answer.

Metals can take a hammering

Metals are **tough**. They do not shatter easily. They do not crack when we hit them or squeeze them. But we can force a metal to bend into a different **shape**. This is easier if the metal is thin.

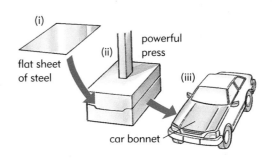

(i) flat sheet of steel
(ii) powerful press
(iii) car bonnet

5 Look at the diagram. Why is steel useful for making car body parts?

Metals don't usually melt easily

Metals are usually **solids**. Only one metal is a liquid at room temperature, but we can melt all metals if we heat them enough. Metals usually have **high** melting points.

Look at the photographs and the table.

6 (a) Which metal is a liquid at room temperature?

(b) Write down <u>one</u> use for this liquid.

7 Which metal is used to make lamp filaments?

8 Which metal has a low melting point, but is a solid at room temperature (20°C)?

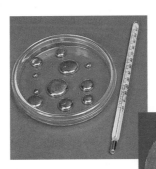

Mercury is a liquid metal.

Temperature of filament is about 2000°C.

Metals are usually strong

Most metals are **strong**. They can hold large weights without snapping.

9 Why do tall buildings have steel frameworks?

Metal	Melting point in °C
mercury	−39
gold	1063
iron	1535
sodium	98
tungsten	3410

What you need to remember [Copy and complete using the **key words**]

What's special about metals?

All metals, except mercury, are _____ at room temperature. Metals usually have _____ melting points. Newly cut metal surfaces are _____.

Metals are good conductors of both _____ and _____.

Metals like steel can carry large weights. We say they are _____.

When you hammer metals:

■ they don't usually break; we say that they are _____

■ they may change their _____.

2 Making the most of metals (1)

Using the properties of metals

The pictures show how we can use the **properties** of metals.

1 Copy out each of the properties (a) to (h) listed below. Then write down the numbers of the pictures that show the property being used. You will need to write down each number more than once.

(a) Most metals are solids at room temperature.

(b) Most metals have high melting points.

(c) Metals are shiny when newly cut or polished.

(d) Most metals are tough.

(e) Most metals are strong.

(f) We can hammer metals into shape.

(g) Metals conduct heat.

(h) Metals conduct electricity.

Using copper

Here are some of the facts about copper:

■ copper is easy to shape into pipes and wires

■ copper pipes and wires are easy to bend

■ copper is a better **conductor** of heat and electricity than most other metals

■ copper is a fairly expensive metal.

2 (a) Write down <u>three</u> uses for copper in our homes.

(b) In each case give a reason for using copper.

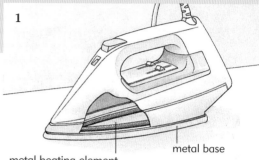

metal heating element   metal base

The steel is shaped to fit the horse's hoof.

The kettle is made from a metal called copper.

metal crane   metal demolition cube

water pipes

Some of the ways we use copper.   electrical **cables**

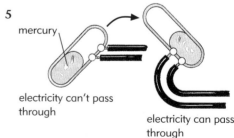

mercury

electricity can't pass through

electricity can pass through

This switch goes on and off when you tilt it.

How can we make copper harder?

A problem with copper is that it is quite a soft metal. This means that it is easily scratched and damaged. We can make it **harder** by mixing it with tin or zinc.

A mixture of different metals is called an **alloy**.

3 Copy and complete the following sentences.

Brass is an alloy of _____ and _____.
Bronze is an alloy of _____ and _____.

4 (a) Bronze is better than copper for knives. Why?

(b) Brass is better than copper for the pins of electric plugs. Why is this?

copper + zinc ⟶ brass

copper + tin ⟶ bronze

Copper in coins

Coins were once made of pure copper, silver or gold. Now coins are made of alloys. 'Silver' coloured coins like a 10p piece are made from an alloy of copper and nickel. A 1p coin is made of steel with a copper coating.

5 Why do you think that we now make coins out of mixtures of metals instead of single metals like copper, silver and gold?

gold and silver are very expensive metals

a copper coin gradually goes darker in air

steel goes rusty quite quickly

What you need to remember [Copy and complete using the **key words**]

Making the most of metals (1)

We use metals when they have the right _____ for the job we want them to do. For example, copper is used in electrical _____ because it is a good _____ of electricity.

We can change the properties of a metal by mixing it with other metals. This mixture is called an _____.

Mixing copper with zinc or tin makes alloys that are _____ than copper.

3 Making the most of metals (2)

Using aluminium

Aluminium is a very **lightweight** metal, and it does not easily corrode. These two properties make aluminium an important metal.

But pure aluminium is weak and soft and easy to bend. This means that we can't use it for many jobs. We can mix aluminium with another light metal called magnesium. We get an alloy that is **stronger**, **harder** and stiffer than aluminium.

1 Write down <u>one</u> use of aluminium

(a) that depends on aluminium being easy to bend

(b) that depends on aluminium being lightweight

(c) that needs an alloy of aluminium.

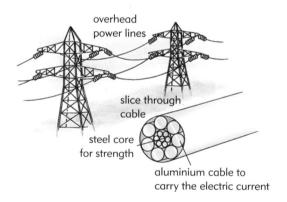

An aeroplane made from aluminium is very light. The metal foil used in cooking has to bend easily.

A ladder needs to be strong and stiff.

Aluminium conducts electricity

Aluminium is a very good **conductor** of electricity. It isn't quite as good as copper but it is much lighter than copper. So it is used for overhead power cables. Steel is much stronger than aluminium, but doesn't conduct electricity so well.

The diagram shows what overhead power cables are made of.

2 What are the cables made from

(a) on the outside? (b) in the centre?

3 Why are the cables made like this?

overhead power lines

slice through cable

steel core for strength

aluminium cable to carry the electric current

Why aluminium doesn't corrode

Metals corrode by reacting with oxygen in the air and water. The metal gets eaten away. For example, when iron rusts it is corroding. This can make metals very weak. The diagram shows why this doesn't happen to aluminium.

4 Copy and complete the following sentences.

A thin layer of _____ _____ forms on the surface of the aluminium. This prevents any further corrosion.

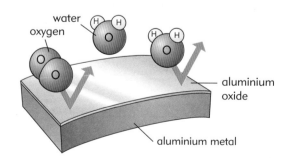

water
oxygen

aluminium oxide

aluminium metal

A tough, thin layer of **aluminium oxide** protects the metal underneath. Water and oxygen cannot get through this layer.

Using steel

Steel is the most widely used metal of all. Millions of tonnes are used every year. Steel is made when iron is mixed with carbon. This makes the metal stronger. Steel is tough and easily shaped. It is also cheaper than most other metals. Vehicle bodies are usually made of steel.

steel supports

steel railway lines

5 Look at the picture. Write down <u>five</u> things in the picture that are usually made from steel.

6 Why is steel used to make so many things?

Making steel even more useful

The bad thing about ordinary steel is that it rusts. We can make **stainless** steel (an alloy) by mixing iron with two other metals called **nickel** and **chromium**. Stainless steel does not rust but it is expensive.

7 Write down <u>three</u> things that we make from stainless steel.

Stainless steel in the kitchen.

What you need to remember [Copy and complete using the **key words**]

Making the most of metals (2)

Aluminium is a very _____ metal.

It is also quite a good _____ of electricity.

Aluminium doesn't corrode because of a tough, thin layer of _____ . _____. Aluminium can be mixed with magnesium. This makes an alloy that is _____ and _____ than aluminium.

Steel is a tough, strong, cheap and easily shaped metal. To stop it rusting we can alloy it with _____ and _____. This is called _____ steel.

[You should be able to give examples of things made from aluminium and steel because of their properties.]

How many metals are there?

Metals, like everything else, are made of very small particles called atoms. A substance that contains just one type of atom is called an element. For example, iron is an element as it contains only iron atoms.

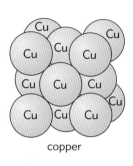

copper

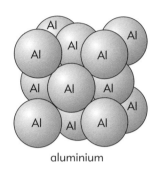

aluminium

1 Write down the names of <u>two</u> other metals that are elements.

How many metal elements are there?

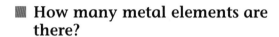

The table shows all of the different elements we find in the natural world around us.

2 (a) How many elements are there altogether?

(b) How many of these elements are metals?

(c) Would you say that about a quarter, about a half or about three-quarters of the elements are metals?

A table of elements set out in this way is called the Periodic Table.

3 What do you notice about where the non-metals and metals are in this table?

Group 1   2

	H
	hydrogen

Li	Be
lithium	beryllium

Na	Mg
sodium	magnesium

Key ▢ metals ▨ non-metals

K	Ca	Sc	Ti	V	Cr	Mn	Fe	C
potassium	calcium	scandium	titanium	vanadium	chromium	manganese	iron	c

Rb	Sr	Y	Zr	Nb	Mo	Tc	Ru	R
rubidium	strontium	yttrium	zirconium	niobium	molybdenum	technetium	ruthenium	rho

Cs	Ba	La*	Hf	Ta	W	Re	Os	
caesium	barium	lanthanum	hafnium	tantalum	tungsten	rhenium	osmium	iri

Fr	Ra	Ac	Th	Pa	U
francium	radium	actinium	thorium	protactinium	uranium

Ce	Pr	Nd	Pm	S
cerium	praseodymium	neodymium	promethium	sam

Melting point (°C) vs % tin / % lead

| | 0 | 10 | 20 | 30 | 40 | 50 | 60 | 70 | 80 | 90 | 100 | % tin |
| | 100 | 90 | 80 | 70 | 60 | 50 | 40 | 30 | 20 | 10 | 0 | % lead |

Periodic table section (groups 3, 4, 5, 6, 7, 0):

3	4	5	6	7	0
					He helium
B boron	C carbon	N nitrogen	O oxygen	F fluorine	Ne neon
Al aluminium	Si silicon	P phosphorus	S sulphur	Cl chlorine	Ar argon

li	Cu copper	Zn zinc	Ga gallium	Ge germanium	As arsenic	Se selenium	Br bromine	Kr krypton
d	Ag silver	Cd cadmium	In indium	Sn tin	Sb antimony	Te tellurium	I iodine	Xe xenon
t	Au gold	Hg mercury	Tl thallium	Pb lead	Bi bismuth	Po polonium	At astatine	Rn radon

*These elements go in here

u	Gd gadolinium	Tb terbium	Dy dysprosium	Ho holmium	Er erbium	Tm thulium	Yb ytterbium	Lu lutetium

Alloys – mixtures of metals

We don't use just the metals that are elements. We also mix metals together to get the properties we want to use. These mixtures of metals are called **alloys**.

Alloys melt at temperatures different from pure metals. Mixtures of lead and tin make solder, which is used to join metals. You can melt it with a soldering iron.

4 Look at the graph of different tin–lead alloys.

(a) What happens to the melting point of the alloy as you add more and more tin to it?

(b) What is the lowest melting point you can get?

(c) What mixture of tin and lead gives you the lowest melting point?

(d) What can these mixtures of tin and lead be used for?

Alloys are usually harder and stronger than the metals from which they are made. Brass is an alloy of copper and zinc. Aluminium is often alloyed with magnesium.

5 (a) How is brass different from copper?

(b) How is the aluminium alloy different from aluminium?

What you need to remember [Copy and complete using the **key words**]

How many metals are there?

About three-quarters of the elements are _____.
You can mix these to make metals called _____.

What's special about non-metals?

Non-metals in your body

Non-metals are just as important to us as metals. We are made mainly of non-metals! The diagram shows the main elements in our bodies.

1 Copy and complete the following sentences.

About ___ per cent of the elements in our bodies are non-metals.

About ___ per cent of the elements in our bodies are metals.

The most common metal in our bodies is _____.

How can we tell if an element is a non-metal?

If the element is a gas at room temperature, then we are sure that it is a non-metal. Look at the bar chart.

2 (a) How many non-metals are gases?

(b) What fraction is this of all the non-metal elements?

If the elements are solids then we look for other clues.

Nearly all solid non-metals crumble or snap or shatter if you hit them or try to bend them. We say that they are **brittle**. Solid non-metals usually look **dull**.

Non-metals are usually **poor** conductors of heat and **electricity**. Solid non-metals usually melt at **low** temperatures. We say they have low melting points.

3 Look at the diagrams. Write down <u>four</u> reasons for thinking that sulphur is a non-metal.

> ### REMEMBER
>
> Most of the elements are metals. The rest of the elements are non-metals.
>
> About one-**quarter** of all the natural elements are non-metals.

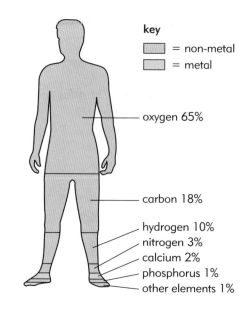

key
▨ = non-metal
▨ = metal

oxygen 65%

carbon 18%

hydrogen 10%
nitrogen 3%
calcium 2%
phosphorus 1%
other elements 1%

Non-metal elements

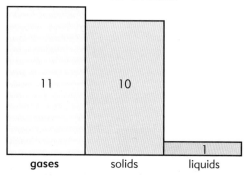

| 11 | 10 | 1 |
| gases | solids | liquids |

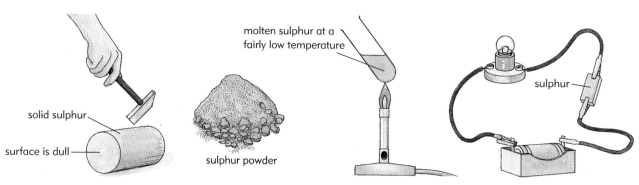

solid sulphur

surface is dull

sulphur powder

molten sulphur at a fairly low temperature

sulphur

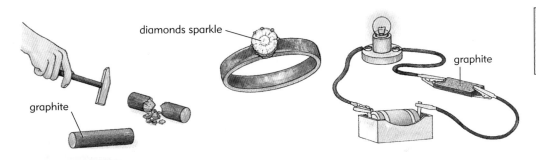

diamonds sparkle

graphite

graphite

Graphite and diamond don't melt even when they are white hot (more than 2000°C).

Carbon is an unusual non-metal

Carbon is an important and unusual non-metal. All known life is based on it. Carbon has two different forms, diamond and graphite.

4 Write down <u>three</u> reasons why carbon is unusual for a non-metal.

5 Write down <u>one</u> reason for thinking that graphite is a non-metal.

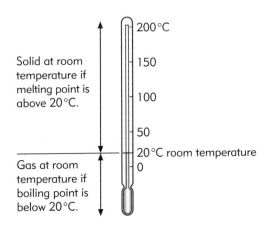

Solid at room temperature if melting point is above 20°C.

Gas at room temperature if boiling point is below 20°C.

200°C

150

100

50

20°C room temperature
0

Solid or gas?

A liquid non-metal

Only one non-metal is a liquid at room temperature. This is **bromine**. Like other non-metals it is a poor conductor of heat and electricity.

6 Mercury is a liquid metal. Write down <u>one</u> thing you would expect mercury but not bromine to do.

Other non-metals – solids or gases?

The table shows the melting points and boiling points of some non-metals.

7 Which <u>two</u> of the elements in the table are solids at room temperature (20°C)?

Element	Melting point in °C	Boiling point in °C
argon	−189	−186
chlorine	−101	−35
helium	−272	−269
hydrogen	−259	−253
iodine	114	184
neon	−248	−246
nitrogen	−210	−196
oxygen	−218	−183
phosphorus	44	280

What you need to remember [Copy and complete using the **key words**]

What's special about non-metals?

About one-_____ of the elements are non-metals.

Most non-metals have _____ melting points.

Half of the non-metals are _____.

The rest are solids apart from _____, which is a liquid.

Solid non-metals usually look _____. They usually break or crumble when we hit them; we say they are _____.

They are usually _____ conductors of heat and _____.

15

Metals

Burning metals

Many metals burn. But some metals burn more easily than others.

Iron and steel

The picture shows a sparkler. Each spark is a small grain of iron burning as it shoots through the air. The iron is reacting with **oxygen**. This reaction gives out heat and light energy.

We can write a <u>word</u> <u>equation</u> for this reaction.

iron + oxygen ⟶ iron oxide + energy

1 Steel is made mainly of iron. Write down an example of where you can see steel burning in air.

2 What new substance is produced when iron burns?

Cutting steel with a very hot flame.

Magnesium

Magnesium burns quickly in the oxygen in the air with a brilliant white flame. The picture shows how we can use this white light.

3 Copy and complete the word equation for the reaction.

magnesium + _____ ⟶ magnesium oxide + energy

4 When you burn magnesium, a white powder is left behind. What is it?

5 Write down a use for the reaction of magnesium with oxygen.

Magnesium is used in flares.

Zinc

Zinc doesn't burn as easily as magnesium. The photographs show how you can make it burn.

6 Copy and complete the word equation for this reaction

_____ + _____ ⟶ _____ + energy

zinc powder

zinc oxide is produced

oxygen

Making zinc oxide.

Metals

Iron and copper

If we heat up iron filings strongly and put them into oxygen, they may glow red-hot and produce a few sparks. Iron oxide powder is produced. Iron burns much less easily than zinc.

If we do the same thing with copper powder there is very little reaction. It just glows a little. Afterwards we see that the surface of the copper has changed from brown to black copper oxide.

7 Write a word equation for

(a) iron burning in oxygen

(b) copper burning in oxygen.

Heating iron filings.

Heating copper powder.

Putting the metals into order

Magnesium burns easily. We say that it is very **reactive**. Zinc does not react so easily with oxygen. It is less reactive than magnesium.

8 Write down the metals copper, iron, magnesium and zinc in order. Start with the most reactive and end with the least reactive.

A list of metals in order of their reactivity is called a reactivity **series**.

most reactive

metal A

metal B

metal C

metal D

least reactive

How to make a reactivity series.

What you need to remember [Copy and complete using the **key words**]

Burning metals

Most metals react with _____.
Some metals react more easily than others; we say that they are more _____.
We can list metals in order of their reactivity. This is called a reactivity _____.

Reacting metals with water

Water consists of hydrogen atoms joined to oxygen atoms. If a metal is reactive enough it can push the hydrogen out of water. We say that the metal **displaces** the hydrogen from water.

1 We sometimes write H_2O instead of water. Explain why.

This is the smallest bit of water – a molecule.

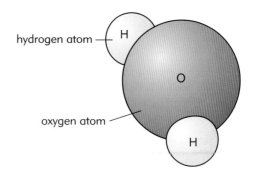

Another way of writing this is H_2O.
This is the formula for water.

▥ Comparing calcium and magnesium

The diagrams show calcium and magnesium reacting with water.

2 Which metal reacts faster with water?

3 (a) What gas is produced in the reactions?

(b) How can you show that this gas is produced?

(c) What other substances are produced in the reactions?

4 Copy and complete the word equation.

calcium + water $\longrightarrow$ _____ + _____

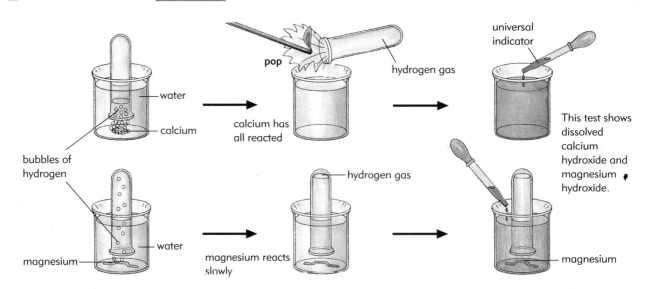

Metals

Making magnesium react faster

If you want to make the magnesium react faster with the water molecules, you can heat the magnesium in steam. Then the magnesium burns in the steam, producing heat and light energy.

Will zinc, iron and copper react with steam?

None of these metals can displace hydrogen from cold water. None of these metals burns in steam as brightly as magnesium does.

The table shows what happens if we try to react them with steam.

5 Write a word equation for the reaction of zinc with steam.

6 Why is copper used to make water pipes and hot water cylinders?

	What happens in steam	What the reaction produces
zinc powder	reacts when heated gently	zinc oxide + hydrogen
iron filings	reacts when heated very strongly	iron oxide + hydrogen
copper powder	no reaction	—

The reactivity series again

7 Write down the metals calcium, copper, iron, magnesium and zinc in order of their reactivity with water.

A metal that is more reactive than hydrogen will displace hydrogen from water. A metal which is less reactive than hydrogen cannot displace hydrogen from water. Very reactive metals displace hydrogen from cold water. Less reactive metals need hot water or steam.

8 Put hydrogen in the right place in your reactivity series.

most reactive

least reactive

This should go alongside your **reactivity** series.

What you need to remember [Copy and complete using the **key words**]

Reacting metals with water

We can put metals into a _____ series according to how easily they react with _____.

We can also put hydrogen into the reactivity series. A metal that is more reactive than hydrogen _____ hydrogen from water.

If you apply a flame to a test tube of hydrogen, it burns with a squeaky

_____.

Reacting metals with acids

Acids like hydrochloric acid and sulphuric acid dissolve many metals. All acids contain hydrogen. The metal pushes the **hydrogen** out of the acid. We say that the metal displaces the hydrogen from the acid, so the reaction is called a displacement reaction.

A metal that displaces hydrogen from an acid is more **reactive** than hydrogen. A metal that does not displace hydrogen from an acid is less reactive than hydrogen.

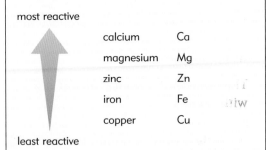

REMEMBER

You can make a reactivity series by:

- seeing how well metals burn

- seeing how well metals react with water

most reactive

calcium	Ca
magnesium	Mg
zinc	Zn
iron	Fe
copper	Cu

least reactive

The diagrams show how four different metals react with dilute acid. The metals are all in powder form.

1 Write down the reactivity series for the four metals shown reacting with acid in the diagrams.

2 Put hydrogen in the right place on your reactivity series.

3 How does the reactivity series for metals reacting with acids compare to the series for metals reacting with oxygen and with water?

4 It isn't safe to react calcium with acid. Why not?

iron
(slow reaction)

copper
(no reaction)

magnesium
(very fast reaction)

zinc
(fast reaction)

Here is the word equation for a reaction with magnesium.

magnesium + hydrochloric acid $\longrightarrow$ magnesium chloride + hydrogen

Here is another way to write the reaction.

$$Mg(s) \quad + \quad 2HCl(aq) \quad \longrightarrow \quad MgCl_2(aq) \quad + \quad H_2(g)$$

| magnesium (a <u>s</u>olid) | hydrochloric acid (<u>aq</u>ueous – this means dissolved in water) | magnesium chloride (<u>aq</u>ueous) | hydrogen (a gas) |

This is called a symbol equation.

---

5 (a) Write a word equation for the reaction between zinc and dilute hydrochloric acid.

   (b) Write a symbol equation for this reaction.

▓ Some very unreactive metals

Silver, gold and platinum are below copper in the reactivity series.

6 What would you expect to happen to these metals in dilute acid? Give a reason for your answer.

most reactive

copper

silver

gold

platinum

least reactive

▓ Some very reactive metals

Potassium and sodium are higher than calcium in the reactivity series.

7 Reacting sodium or potassium with water can be dangerous. Why is this?

dilute acid

silver

gold

platinum

most reactive

potassium

sodium

calcium

least reactive

▓ Understanding symbol equations

This symbol equation describes the reaction of sodium with water.

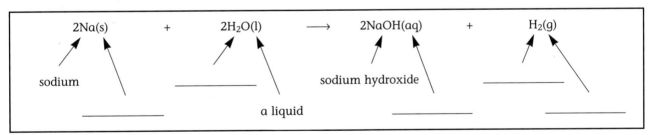

$$2Na(s) \quad + \quad 2H_2O(l) \quad \longrightarrow \quad 2NaOH(aq) \quad + \quad H_2(g)$$

sodium

a liquid

sodium hydroxide

_____

_____

_____

_____

For the moment, don't worry about what the numbers mean.

8 Make a large, well-spread-out copy of the symbol equation. Underneath write what each part of the equation tells you.

What you need to remember [Copy and complete using the **key words**]

Reacting metals with acids

Some metals react with dilute acids; _____ gas is produced. This reaction happens with metals that are more _____ than hydrogen.

Competing metals

The photographs show what happens when you put an iron nail into copper sulphate solution.

1 Copy and complete the following sentences.

The iron nail becomes coated with _____.
The liquid changes colour from _____
to _____.
The liquid has changed from _____ sulphate
solution to _____ sulphate solution.

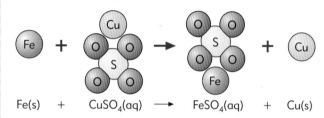

$$Fe(s) \quad + \quad CuSO_4(aq) \longrightarrow FeSO_4(aq) \quad + \quad Cu(s)$$

2 Write down a word equation for this reaction.

Iron is more reactive than copper. The iron pushes the copper out of the copper sulphate solution. We say that the iron has **displaced** the copper.

Which metals compete best?

A more reactive metal usually **displaces** a **less** reactive metal from a solution of one of its compounds.

3 Look at the photographs. Which is the more reactive metal?

4 We say that the magnesium _____ the copper from the copper sulphate.

5 Write a word equation to describe this reaction.

Using the reactivity series

You can use the reactivity series to predict whether a displacement reaction will happen.

6 Copy the table. Use the short reactivity series to decide whether a displacement reaction will happen. Fill in the missing ticks and crosses.

Put a tick if you think a reaction will happen and a cross if you think it won't.

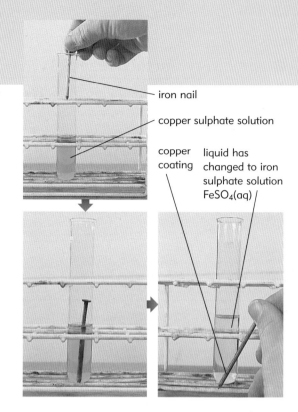

iron nail

copper sulphate solution

copper coating

liquid has changed to iron sulphate solution $FeSO_4(aq)$

magnesium   copper

no change

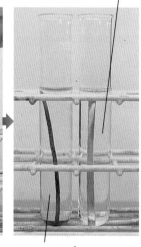

copper sulphate   magnesium sulphate

now magnesium sulphate solution

most reactive

magnesium	Mg
iron	Fe
copper	Cu

least reactive

	Magnesium sulphate solution	Iron sulphate solution	Copper sulphate solution
Mg			✓
Fe			✓
Cu	✗		

Pushing a metal out of its solid compound

Aluminium is more reactive than iron. So if you heat up aluminium powder with iron oxide there is a reaction.

$$2Al(s) + Fe_2O_3(s) \longrightarrow Al_2O_3(s) + 2Fe(l)$$

7 Write a word equation for this reaction.

When the reaction starts, it makes so much heat that the iron is melted. The photograph shows this reaction being used to weld together railway lines. The welders build a small mould around the gap between the railway lines. The molten iron runs down into the gap and welds the two sections together.

8 The welders who carry out this reaction stand back at a distance from the reaction and wear thick heatproof gloves. Why is this?

A non-metal that can push out metals

Carbon isn't a **metal**, but if we heat it up, it can displace less reactive metals from their oxides. This is why we put it in the **reactivity** series.

9 Carbon will displace only those metals below it in the reactivity series. Will carbon displace:

(a) aluminium from aluminium oxide?

(b) iron from iron oxide?

most reactive

potassium	K
sodium	Na
calcium	Ca
magnesium	Mg
aluminium	Al
carbon	C
zinc	Zn
iron	Fe
tin	Sn
lead	Pb
hydrogen	H
copper	Cu
silver	Ag
gold	Au
platinum	Pt

least reactive

Putting all the previous reactivity series together. The non-metals are underlined.

What you need to remember [Copy and complete using the **key words**]

Competing metals

A more reactive metal will push a _____ reactive metal out of its compounds. We say that it _____ the less reactive metal.
We can also put carbon into the _____ series because it can displace a less reactive _____ from a metal oxide.

10 Where do metals come from?

■ Where do we find metals?

We find metals mixed with rocks in the Earth's **crust**. We find gold in the Earth's crust as the metal itself. The pieces of gold in rocks contain just gold and nothing else. You can collect lots of small pieces of gold, heat them until they melt and then pour the molten gold into a mould. The gold sets hard as it cools. Gold is a very rare metal. Many other metals are much more common than gold.

1 Which are the <u>two</u> most common metals in the Earth's crust?

2 Why don't we show gold in the pie chart?

We find most metals, including iron and aluminium, as metal **ores**. In the ore, the metal is joined with other **elements**. Metals are often joined with oxygen in compounds we call metal **oxides**. For example, most iron ores contain iron oxide. Metals may also be joined with sulphur in compounds we call metal sulphides.

■ Looking at ores

The photograph shows a common iron ore.

3 (a) What is the name of this iron ore?

   (b) There are <u>two</u> elements in the ore, what are they?

Look at the photographs showing two other metal ores.

4 Copy the headings and then complete the table.

Name of the ore	Metal in the ore	Other elements in the ore

malachite is copper carbonate

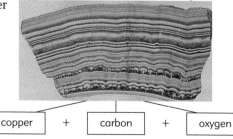

copper	+	carbon	+	oxygen

REMEMBER

A more reactive element will displace (push out) a less reactive metal from one of its compounds.

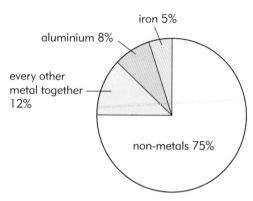

iron 5%
aluminium 8%
every other metal together 12%
non-metals 75%

Elements in the Earth's crust. Gold makes up only three parts in every thousand million parts of the Earth's crust.

iron ore often contains haematite, a type of iron oxide

haematite

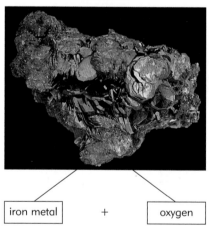

iron metal	+	oxygen

galena is lead sulphide

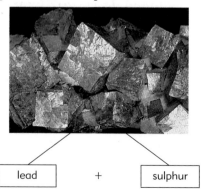

lead	+	sulphur

How can we release metals from their ores?

To get pure metals from ores you must split up the metal compound in the ore. You can release, or extract, some metals by heating the metal oxide with **carbon**.

We can extract copper by heating copper oxide with charcoal, a form of carbon. The charcoal reacts with the oxygen in the copper oxide. This leaves copper metal.

5 (a) What other substance is produced?

    (b) Write a word equation for this reaction.

Removing oxygen from a metal oxide is called **reduction**. So carbon has reduced the copper oxide. Reducing iron oxide with carbon needs a much higher temperature than for copper. Aluminium oxide cannot be split using carbon. Aluminium oxide can be reduced to aluminium metal only by using **electricity**.

6 Use the reactivity series to explain why:

    (a) You can't reduce aluminium oxide using carbon.

    (b) It is harder to reduce iron oxide than copper oxide.

    (c) Gold is the metal itself in the Earth's crust.

How much metal is there in metal ores?

Metal ores contain rock as well as the valuable metal compounds. Different ores contain different amounts of rock.

7 How much metal compound is there in 100 g of each of the ores shown?

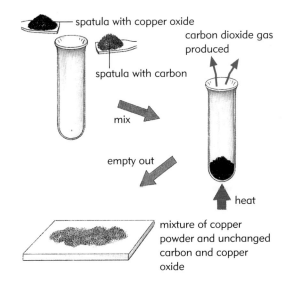

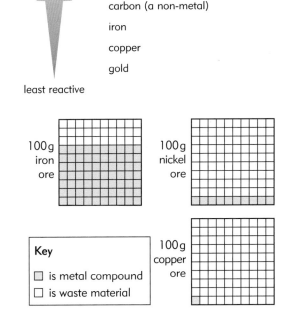

What you need to remember [Copy and complete using the **key words**]

Where do metals come from?

Metals are found in the Earth's _____.
Most metals, except gold, are found joined with other _____ as compounds.
Compounds of metals and oxygen are called _____.
Rocks containing metal compounds are called _____.
Copper and iron are extracted from their oxides by heating them with _____.
Removing the oxygen from a metal oxide is called _____.
Aluminium oxide can only be reduced using _____.

How do we get all the steel we use?

Steel is a strong and tough material. It is also cheap to make. Steel is mostly iron, so to make steel, we must first extract iron from iron ore.

How can you get iron from iron ore?

We extract iron from iron ore in a **blast** furnace.

1 Look at the diagram of the blast furnace.

   (a) Write down the <u>four</u> things that go into the blast furnace.

   (b) Write down the <u>three</u> things that come out of the blast furnace.

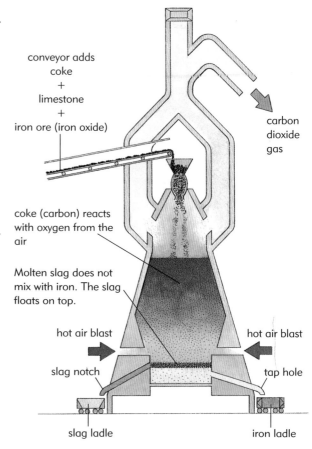

conveyor adds
coke
+
limestone
+
iron ore (iron oxide)

carbon dioxide gas

coke (carbon) reacts with oxygen from the air

Molten slag does not mix with iron. The slag floats on top.

hot air blast

hot air blast

slag notch

tap hole

slag ladle

iron ladle

tap hole – molten iron comes out here
slag notch – molten slag comes out here

Why is coke needed in the blast furnace?

First the **coke** reacts with oxygen from the **air** to make carbon **dioxide** gas. This reaction releases lots of heat.

$$C(s) + O_2(g) \longrightarrow CO_2(g) + energy$$

2 Write down a word equation for this reaction.

Next the carbon dioxide reacts with hot coke to give carbon **monoxide** gas.

$$CO_2(g) + C(s) \longrightarrow 2CO(g)$$

3 Write down a word equation for this reaction.

4 What are the <u>two</u> different jobs that coke does inside the blast furnace?

The carbon monoxide **reduces** the iron oxide to give iron metal. Carbon **dioxide** gas is also made at the same time.

carbon monoxide + iron oxide → iron + carbon dioxide

The hot air that is blasted into the furnace contains both oxygen and nitrogen gases. Nitrogen is not a **reactive** gas, so it goes through the furnace without changing. Oxygen is reactive, and joins with carbon to make carbon dioxide gas.

5 Which gases will be in the waste gases that come out of the top of the furnace?

Carbon is above iron in the reactivity series.

most reactive

aluminium

carbon

zinc

iron

least reactive

So carbon can be used to reduce iron oxide.

▥ Why is limestone needed in the blast furnace?

Iron ore contains solid waste, such as sand, as well as the useful iron oxide. This waste would make the iron weak so it must be removed. **Limestone** reacts with the solid waste to produce **slag**. The blast furnace is so hot that both the iron and slag **melt** and trickle down to the base where they collect.

6 How are the molten iron and slag removed from the base of the furnace?

7 Why is it easy to keep the iron separate from the slag?

8 Write down <u>two</u> reasons why a blast furnace needs to be very hot.

▥ What is the difference between iron and steel?

Most of the iron made in the blast furnace is turned into steel. The table shows some of the differences between iron and mild steel.

Material	% carbon	Properties of the material
iron from the blast furnace	4.0	brittle, hard
mild steel	0.4	bends easily, can be rolled into thin sheets

9 Why do you think that mild steel is a more useful material than iron from the blast furnace?

10 How does the amount of carbon in mild steel compare with that in iron from the blast furnace?

What you need to remember [Copy and complete using the **key words**]

How do we get all the steel we use?

Iron is extracted from iron ore in a _____ furnace.

The high temperature needed is produced by burning _____ in the hot _____ that is blasted into the furnace. This makes carbon _____ gas.

The carbon dioxide then reacts with more carbon to make carbon _____ gas.

Carbon is more _____ than iron, so carbon monoxide takes the oxygen from iron oxide. This gives the metal iron and a gas called carbon _____.

The carbon monoxide _____ the iron oxide to iron metal.

Solid waste materials in the iron ore react with _____ to make _____.

The furnace is so hot that the iron and slag both _____ and run down to the base of the furnace.

Using electricity to split up metal compounds

We can get some metals from their ores by heating them with carbon.

Another way to get metals from their compounds is to pass **electricity** through the compound.

> **REMEMBER**
>
> Solid metals and graphite let electricity pass through them. Solid metal compounds such as metal ores do not conduct electricity.

1 What is the problem with trying to pass electricity through metal compounds?

To make a metal compound conduct electricity we must either **melt** it or **dissolve** it.

Getting copper from copper chloride

Copper chloride is a metal compound that dissolves in water. The diagram shows what happens when an electric current passes through copper chloride solution.

2 Copy and complete the word equation.

copper chloride $\xrightarrow{\text{electricity}}$ _____ + _____

3 Copy and complete the following sentences.

Copper is produced at the _____ electrode.

Chlorine gas is produced at the _____ electrode.

The electricity has split up the copper chloride. We say that the copper chloride has been **decomposed**.

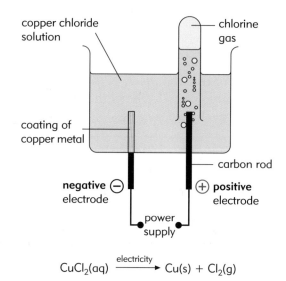

$$CuCl_2(aq) \xrightarrow{\text{electricity}} Cu(s) + Cl_2(g)$$

Getting lead from lead bromide

Lead bromide is another metal compound, but it does not dissolve in water. To make electricity pass through lead bromide you must first melt it.

The diagram shows what happens when you melt lead bromide and pass an electric current through it.

4 Write down a word equation for this reaction.

When we split up a compound by passing an electric current through it, we call it **electrolysis**.

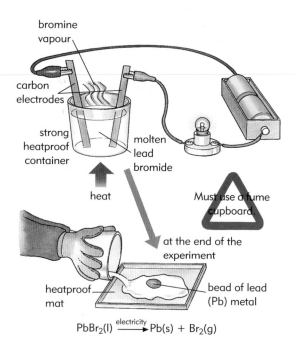

$$PbBr_2(l) \xrightarrow{\text{electricity}} Pb(s) + Br_2(g)$$

▨ How does electrolysis work?

In copper chloride solution:

▪ the copper atoms have a positive (+) charge

▪ the chlorine atoms have a negative (–) charge.

Electrically charged atoms are called **ions**. When we dissolve solid copper chloride in water, the ions can **move** about.

Look at the diagrams.

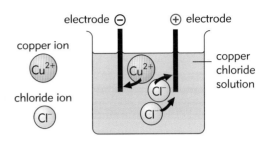

5 Copy and complete the following sentences.

The copper ions have a _____ charge.

They move to the _____ electrode.

The chloride ions have a _____ charge.

They move to the _____ electrode.

This shows that opposite charges _____.

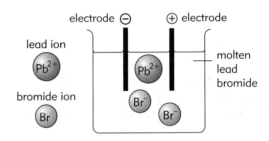

The ions move to the electrode with the opposite charge. Opposite charges attract.

Lead bromide is made of charged ions. We call it an ionic compound. When we melt solid lead bromide, the ions can then move about.

6 Copy the diagram showing lead bromide. Mark on the diagram the way that the ions move during electrolysis.

Metal compounds are ionic. Look at the table of ions.

7 Copy and complete the following sentence.

During electrolysis metals are always formed at the _____ electrode.

Metal ions	Non-metal ions
sodium Na^+	chloride Cl^-
copper Cu^{2+}	bromide Br^-
lead Pb^{2+}	oxide O^{2-}
aluminium Al^{3+}	

Metal ions always have a positive charge.

What you need to remember [Copy and complete using the **key words**]

Using electricity to split up metal compounds

Electrically charged atoms are called _____.
You can split up a metal compound by passing _____ through it.
You can do this only if you _____ the compound by heating it, or
_____ the compound in water.
This means that the ions in the compound can _____ about.
Using electricity to split up a compound is called _____. We say that the
compound has been _____.
The metal ions in a compound have a _____ charge.
During electrolysis, the metal ions always move towards the _____ electrode.

13 How do we get all the aluminium we need?

Aluminium is the most common metal in the Earth's crust. But you never find pieces of natural aluminium. This is because aluminium is a very reactive metal. Aluminium combines with other elements to form compounds.

Look at the photograph.

1 What is the name of natural aluminium ore?

2 Which aluminium compound do you find in aluminium ore?

3 Clay contains aluminium compounds. Why don't we extract aluminium from clay?

How do we get aluminium from its ore?

We use carbon to extract iron from iron oxide, but we cannot use carbon to extract aluminium from aluminium **oxide**. It doesn't work.

Look at the reactivity series.

4 Why can't carbon push aluminium out of aluminium oxide?

We must extract aluminium in a different way. We need to use electricity to extract aluminium from its oxide. We must make the aluminium ore conduct electricity to do this.

How to make aluminium oxide conduct electricity

Aluminium oxide does not dissolve in water to give a solution, so to make it conduct we have to melt it.

Look at the diagrams.

5 What is the problem with melting aluminium oxide?

6 How can we solve the problem?

When we have melted aluminium oxide we can use electricity to split it up. This is called electrolysis.

> **REMEMBER**
>
> Solid metal compounds will not conduct electricity. We have to melt them or dissolve them in water.

We get aluminium from bauxite ore. Bauxite is a form of aluminium oxide.

| aluminium | + | oxygen |

A lot of aluminium in the Earth's crust is in clay. It is very hard to get the aluminium from the clay.

most reactive

aluminium

carbon

zinc

iron

least reactive

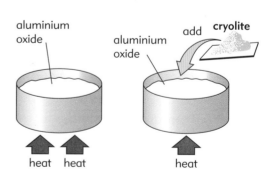

To melt the aluminium oxide you need to heat it to a **high** temperature, more than 2000 °C. This is much hotter than a Bunsen burner flame.

A mixture of cryolite and aluminium oxide melts at a lower temperature of 950 °C.

Using electrolysis to split up aluminium oxide

The diagram shows how aluminium is made from melted aluminium oxide.

7 (a) What two materials does aluminium oxide give when it splits up?

   (b) Write down where each of these materials is formed.

8 (a) What do we use to make the electrodes?

   (b) The positive electrode burns away and we must replace it with a new one. Write down why it burns away.

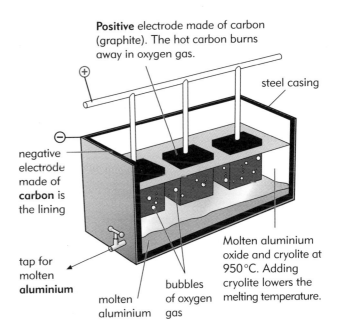

Positive electrode made of carbon (graphite). The hot carbon burns away in oxygen gas.

steel casing

negative electrode made of **carbon** is the lining

tap for molten **aluminium**

molten aluminium

bubbles of oxygen gas

Molten aluminium oxide and cryolite at 950°C. Adding cryolite lowers the melting temperature.

Why does electrolysis work?

In aluminium oxide both the aluminium and the oxygen have electrical charges. We call them aluminium ions and oxide ions. If you melt aluminium oxide, the ions can move about in the liquid.

9 Copy and complete the following sentences.

   Aluminium ions have a _____ charge.

   They move to the _____ electrode.

   Oxide ions have a _____ charge.

   They move to the _____ electrode.

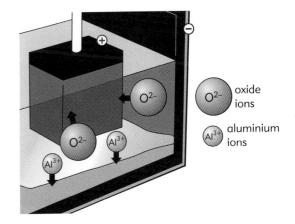

O^{2-} oxide ions

Al^{3+} aluminium ions

What you need to remember [Copy and complete using the **key words**]

How do we get all the aluminium we need?

We can extract aluminium from the compound aluminium _____.
Aluminium oxide melts at a very _____ temperature.
We can lower the melting temperature by adding a substance called _____.
The electrodes are made of _____.
Since the temperature is high and oxygen is given off, the _____ electrode burns away.
Molten _____ collects at the base.

31

Metals

Metals through the ages

The diagram shows lots of different things about metals.

1 Copy and complete the following sentences.

The first metal that people found and used was _____.

This metal is the _____ reactive.

2 How long ago were copper, iron and aluminium first used?

Explain your answer.

The alkali metals sodium and potassium were first discovered by Sir Humphry Davy in 1807.

3 Why do you think the alkali metals were not discovered much earlier?

Most metals react with oxygen or water. This makes them corrode.

4 Copy and complete the following sentences.

The most reactive metals usually corrode _____.

The least reactive metals usually corrode _____.

5 (a) Which metal corrodes more slowly than you would expect?

(b) Explain why this happens.

Dates	Metals and their use
about 50 years ago (plenty of cheap electricity)	Aluminium is used to make many things, including aeroplanes.
about 200 years ago (Volta invented the battery, which produced an electric current)	[alkali metals discovered]
IRON AGE	Steel is harder and tougher than bronze.
4,000 years ago	
BRONZE AGE	Bronze is mainly copper, with tin added to make it harder.
6,000 years ago	Jewellery and coins were made from gold.
STONE AGE	
10,000 years ago	Tools were made from stone.

How the metal is extracted	Reactivity	How quickly the metals corrode
By passing an electric current though the molten metal compound.	MOST REACTIVE alkali metals aluminium	FASTEST CORROSION alkali metals In damp air … freshly cut sodium or potassium … … starts to corrode in seconds.
By heating iron oxide with carbon in a very hot furnace.	[carbon] iron	iron … a shiny, new iron nail … … starts to corrode in hours or days.
By heating copper oxide with carbon.	copper	copper … a shiny, new copper coin … … starts to corrode in weeks or months. aluminium … aluminium quickly gets a coating of aluminium oxide, which is very tough and stops further corrosion.
You find gold as the metal in the ground.	gold LEAST REACTIVE	gold … gold does not corrode. SLOWEST CORROSION

What you need to remember

Metals through the ages

There are no new things to remember on these two pages.
They bring together ideas from a lot of other pages.

Which ores should we mine?

Many rocks contain metal compounds, but most rocks are no use as ores. They do not contain enough metal so it costs too much to extract the metal. We say that it is not <u>economic</u> to use the rocks as ores.

1 Look at the information on the bar charts.

Then copy and complete the table.

Metal	What 1 kg of the metal is worth	Amount of metal in ore worth using
lead		
copper		
gold		

The more valuable a metal is, the less there needs to be in rocks to make them worth using as ores.

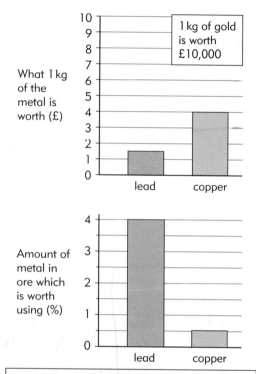

What 1 kg of the metal is worth (£)

1 kg of gold is worth £10,000

lead   copper

Amount of metal in ore which is worth using (%)

lead   copper

Gold is worth mining even if there are only 10 parts in every million. This is about the same amount as 2 wedding rings in a truck-load of rock.

■ Concentrating the metal compounds in ores

Some ores contain only a small amount of metal compound. This needs to be separated from the rest of the rock before the metal can be extracted from it. The diagram shows one way of doing this.

2 Copy and complete the following sentences.

A crusher breaks the ore up into bits of
_____ and bits of _____ _____.

The crushed ore is then churned up with _____,
_____ and _____.

The bits of metal compound are carried away mainly by the _____.

The bits of waste rock are carried away mainly by the _____.

The metal can then be extracted from the concentrated ore.

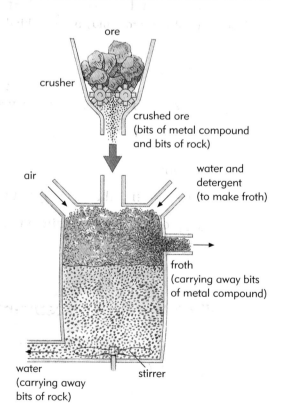

ore

crusher

crushed ore (bits of metal compound and bits of rock)

air

water and detergent (to make froth)

froth (carrying away bits of metal compound)

water (carrying away bits of rock)

stirrer

Metals

Metals and the environment

Iron ore mine in Australia.

Gold mine in Brazil.

Mining metals and metal ores can make huge holes in the Earth's crust.

Huge heaps of waste rock may be left behind.

Wastes still contain metal compounds. These can pollute streams and harm living things.

Without metals, our lives would be very different. There would be no cars, televisions, fridges and many other things. There wouldn't be any electricity either.

But producing these useful metals also causes problems.

3 Write down:

(a) <u>three</u> problems that mining metal ores can cause;

(b) <u>one</u> problem that extracting metals from their ores can cause.

Metal compounds are often heated with carbon to extract the metal. This can pollute the air.

What you need to remember

Which ores should we mine?

You should be able to comment on the economic and environmental aspects of producing metals, just like you have on these pages.

The bad taste guide to acids and alkalis

Have you ever rushed to the bathroom to be sick? Do you remember the burning feeling in your nose and throat? Do you remember the strange 'set on edge' feeling of your teeth and that awful sour taste in your mouth?

If so, then that was your first experience of the chemistry of hydrochloric acid.

1 Write down <u>two</u> things that you know about hydrochloric acid.

Stomach acid kills 99 per cent of all known household germs.

Strong acids

The hydrochloric acid in your stomach is one of your best friends. It helps to digest your food. It is a very strong acid, but luckily your stomach has got an acidproof lining.

All acids **dissolve** in water to give colourless and **corrosive** solutions. Strong acids will harm most living tissue and dissolve or corrode most metals and rocks.

2 Car batteries contain sulphuric acid. This is a very strong acid. Write down <u>two</u> reasons why you must take care not to spill it.

3 Write down the name of a substance that acids will not dissolve.

4 Your stomach normally contains hydrochloric acid, but you should <u>never</u> drink it. Why not?

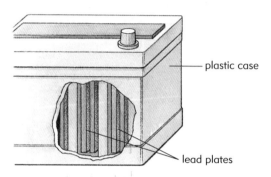

A lead–acid battery.

Weak acids

Most acids are not strong. There are many weak acids in what we eat and drink. These are only slightly corrosive.

5 Write a list of <u>three</u> drinks or foods that taste sour. These contain weak acids.

These things contain weak acids.

Metals

Alkalis – the opposites of acids

Alkalis dissolve in water to form **colourless** solutions. Alkalis usually have a name ending in hydroxide. Two examples are sodium hydroxide and calcium hydroxide.

Like acids, strong alkalis attack living tissue. But unlike acids, they would turn bits of you to soap. If you rub your fingers together with dilute sodium hydroxide, they will feel soapy. This is because the sodium hydroxide turns the fat and oils on the surface of your skin into soap.

Many powerful oven cleaners contain strong alkalis.

6 You should <u>not</u> do this with concentrated sodium hydroxide solution. Why not?

7 Why is it important to wear safety spectacles or goggles when using alkalis?

8 What other protection do you need when using an oven cleaner?

Not an acid, not an alkali

Water is not an acid and not an alkali. Water is **neutral**.

When a substance dissolves in water, it makes an **aqueous** solution. Aqueous means 'watery'. We have seen that we can have aqueous solutions of acids and alkalis. Salt, sugar, alcohol and many other substances dissolve in water to give solutions that are not acidic or alkaline. They are neutral.

9 Look at the three liquids. Explain why you cannot tell which is which just by looking.

The labels have fallen off these three bottles.

What you need to remember [Copy and complete using the **key words**]

The bad taste guide to acids and alkalis

We must handle acids with care because they are _____.
This is especially true when they are strong.
Acids _____ in water to make colourless solutions.
The opposites of acids are _____. These substances are also corrosive.
Alkalis also dissolve in water to give _____ solutions.
Water is neither an acid nor an alkali. It is _____. Many _____ or watery solutions are neutral.

Colour me red when acidic

To taste or not to taste

It's all well and good, saying that acids taste sour. Imagine that you have to find out whether a clear, colourless liquid in your laboratory is an acid, an alkali or water. Tasting it is <u>not</u> a good idea. It could seriously and suddenly shorten your life!

1 Chemists do <u>not</u> taste chemicals. Why not?

Indicators

When a car driver is about to turn left, the driver clicks on the left indicator. The car's left-hand flashing yellow lights tell other road users that the car is going to turn left.

Chemists also use **indicators**. These are dyes that change **colour** with acids and alkalis. Instead of left or right, chemical indicators tell us whether the solution is **acidic** or **alkaline** or neutral.

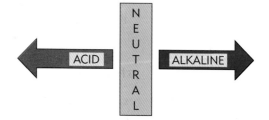

Litmus

Litmus is an indicator. Neutral litmus is purple.

2 Copy and complete the following sentences.

Acids turn litmus _____.

Alkalis turn litmus _____.

3 What colour do you think litmus gives with a neutral liquid like water?

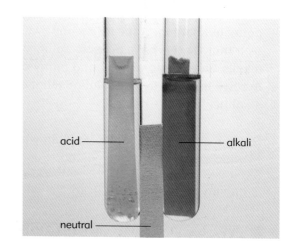

How strong is my acid or alkali?

We use a scale of numbers called the **pH** scale (the 'pee-aitch' scale) to tell us how strong an acid or alkali is. The more acidic the solution is, then the lower the pH number is. The more alkaline the solution is then the higher the pH number is.

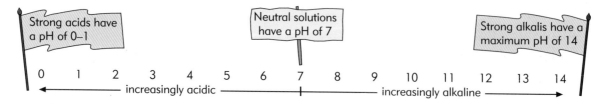

Strong acids have a pH of 0–1

Neutral solutions have a pH of 7

Strong alkalis have a maximum pH of 14

0 1 2 3 4 5 6 7 8 9 10 11 12 13 14

← increasingly acidic — increasingly alkaline →

Metals

Very strong acids have a pH between 0 and 1.
Neutral solutions have a pH of 7.
Strong alkalis have a maximum pH of 14.

Substance	pH
ammonia cleaning liquid	11.5
blood	7.5
coffee	5
liquid X	7
liquid Y	8.5
liquid Z	4
orange juice	3
oven cleaner	14
stomach acid	1.5
urine	6

4   Make a table with these headings.

Substance	pH

Put the substances from the list into your table in order of their pH numbers. Start with the highest pH and go down to the lowest.

5   Underline in red the most acidic substance in your table. Underline the most alkaline substance in purple.

6   Which of the substances in the table is probably water? Underline this in green.

Universal indicator – a chemical rainbow

Universal indicator is a mixture of dyes. Each dye changes colour at a different pH so the mixture gives us different colours as we go through the pH range. We add the indicator in drops, so the chemical we test must be colourless for us to see the proper colour change.

Colour	red			orange		yellow		green	blue		navy blue			purple	
pH	0	1	2	3	4	5	6	7	8	9	10	11	12	13	14

increasingly acidic ⟵   neutral   ⟶ increasingly alkaline

7   Which <u>two</u> substances in your copied table will turn universal indicator orange?

8   Why would it be difficult to test a cup of coffee with universal indicator?

What you need to remember [Copy and complete using the **key words**]

Colour me red when acidic

To show whether solutions are acidic, alkaline or neutral, we use _____.
Indicators are dyes that change _____ in acids or alkalis.
We measure the strength of an acid or alkali by its _____ number.

The pH scale

0   1   2   3   4   5   6   7   8   9   10   11   12   13   14

increasingly _____ ⟵   ↑   ➡ increasingly _____

At pH 7, a solution is _____.

18 Acids and alkalis can cancel each other out

The diagrams show what happens as you add more and more **acid** to an **alkali**.

1 What colour is the indicator in diagram B?

2 Is the solution in the flask in diagram B acidic, alkaline or neutral?

If you add just the right amount of acid to an alkali you get a solution that is neutral. We say that the acid and alkali **neutralise** each other. We call the reaction between an acid and an alkali **neutralisation**.

The table tells you more about how the **indicator** changes colour as you keep on adding acid.

3 Make a copy of the table. Then complete it to show the missing colours.

Volume of acid added (cm³)	Colour of universal indicator
0.0	purple
24.0	navy blue
25.0	
25.5	green
26.0	
27.0	orange
28.0	red

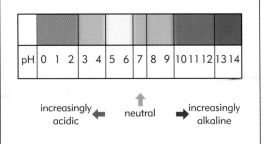

REMEMBER

Universal indicator tells us the pH of a solution.

| pH | 0 | 1 | 2 | 3 | 4 | 5 | 6 | 7 | 8 | 9 | 10 | 11 | 12 | 13 | 14 |

increasingly acidic ← neutral → increasingly alkaline

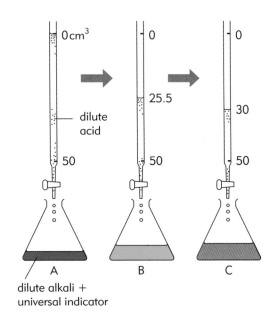

A — dilute alkali + universal indicator

B

C

0 cm³ — dilute acid
25.5
30

▮ Remember the stomach acid?

If you have indigestion, your stomach has probably produced too much acid. Some people take indigestion medicine. This contains very mild alkalis such as magnesium hydroxide. The alkalis neutralise the extra acid.

4 The alkali contained in the indigestion medicine is not very harmful. How do you know this?

5 What colour would you expect the indigestion medicine to show with universal indicator?

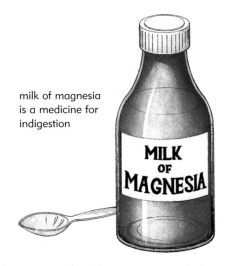

milk of magnesia is a medicine for indigestion

Take one or two tablespoons every six hours as required.

How does your cabbage grow?

Most plants like to grow in soils that have a pH of slightly less than 7. Some garden soils are too acidic. Gardeners use a mild alkali called slaked lime to neutralise garden soil. A few plants, such as cabbage, like the pH to be about 8. Cabbages are lime-loving plants.

6 Look at the photograph.

(a) What is the pH of the soil?

(b) Explain what the gardener should do to make the cabbage grow best.

Buzzingly painful neutralisations

When a bee stings you, it injects an acid into your skin. You can treat bee stings by bathing them with sodium bicarbonate. This is an alkali that neutralises the acid in the sting.

When a wasp stings, it injects an alkali into your skin. You can treat the sting with vinegar. Vinegar contains a weak acid called ethanoic acid. This neutralises the wasp sting.

7 Why is it wrong to treat a bee sting with vinegar?

Bicarbonate for bees. Vinegar for wasps.

Wash-day blues

We normally wash clothes with artificial detergents. Manufacturers make these from molecules found in crude oil. First they turn them into strong acids. Then they neutralise the acids with the alkali, sodium hydroxide. This makes the detergent.

8 Sometimes, by mistake, soap-powder manufacturers make the detergents too acidic. What can happen to your clothes if you wash them in such a detergent?

What you need to remember [Copy and complete using the **key words**]

Acids and alkalis can cancel each other out

When we add an acid to an alkali they _____ each other.

This reaction is called _____.

An acid will neutralise an _____.

An alkali will neutralise an _____.

We can check whether neutralisation has taken place by using an _____.

Neutralisation – where do the acid and alkali go?

When you mix some acid with just the right amount of alkali you get a neutral solution. But all the particles from the acid and alkali are still there. They have reacted to make new substances.

1 What does the indicator tell you about these new substances?

We can then repeat the neutralisation without using the indicator. We don't need the indicator now, because we already know how much acid to use.

2 What new substance does the neutral solution contain?

The reaction also makes more water.

3 Copy and complete the word equation for this reaction.

sodium hydroxide + hydrochloric acid $\longrightarrow$ _____ + _____

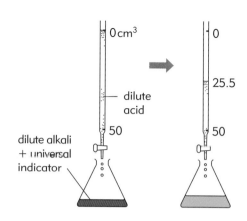

Neutralising sodium hydroxide with hydrochloric acid.

▨ Different kinds of salt

Sodium chloride is the salt you put on your food. But it isn't the only kind of salt. Whenever you neutralise an acid with an alkali you get a **salt** and **water**.

4 Copy and complete the word equation.

Any _____ + any _____ $\longrightarrow$ a salt + water

5 Look at the photograph. Write down the names of <u>three</u> different kinds of salt besides common salt.

▨ How do you know which salt you have made?

When you neutralise **hydrochloric** acid, the salt you make is always a chloride. The salt takes the first part of its name from the metal in the alkali you use. So neutralising **sodium** hydroxide with hydrochloric acid gives you sodium chloride.

6 What salt do you get if you neutralise potassium hydroxide with hydrochloric acid?

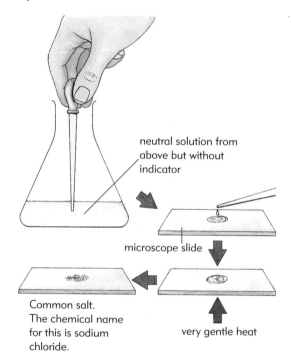

Common salt. The chemical name for this is sodium chloride.

All these substances are salts.

Metals

The salts of **nitric** acid are nitrates.
The salts of **sulphuric** acid are sulphates.

7 Copy and complete the word equations.

(a) potassium sulphuric ⟶ _____
    hydroxide + acid   _____ + water

(b) _____ + _____ ⟶ sodium + water
       hydroxide   acid   nitrate

■ Making a salt

The diagrams show how to make **potassium** chloride.

8 Write down the following steps in the right order –
  the first two steps are done for you.

  Measure out some dilute hydrochloric acid.
  Add a few drops of litmus indicator.

  ■ Heat the colourless solution in the evaporating
    basin almost to dryness.

  ■ Stop when the solution is neutral – the litmus goes
    from red to purple.

  ■ Add dilute potassium hydroxide a bit at a time.

  ■ Boil the purple solution with charcoal to remove
    the litmus.

  ■ Filter off the charcoal, putting the colourless
    solution produced into an evaporating basin.

  ■ Leave the evaporating basin to cool.

9 Write a word equation for the neutralisation.

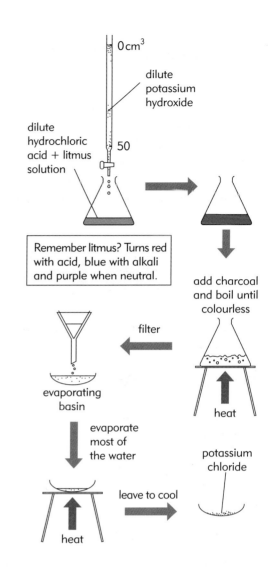

Making potassium chloride. The symbol
equation for the neutralisation at the start is:

$KOH(aq) + HCl(aq) \longrightarrow KCl(aq) + H_2O(l)$

What you need to remember [Copy and complete using the **key words**]

Neutralisation – where do the acid and alkali go?

Acid + alkali ⟶ _____ + _____

To make:

■ a sodium salt you use _____ hydroxide with an acid

■ a potassium salt you use _____ hydroxide with an acid

■ a chloride you use _____ acid with an alkali

■ a nitrate you use _____ acid with an alkali

■ a sulphate you use _____ acid with an alkali

Making some acids and alkalis from elements

You can make acids from some non-metal elements, if the elements are reacted first to make **oxides**.
You can make alkalis from some metal elements.

Making an acid from sulphur

The diagram shows how you can make an acidic solution starting from the element sulphur.

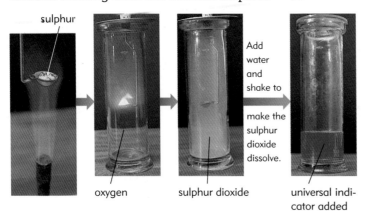

sulphur

oxygen   sulphur dioxide   universal indi-
                                             cator added

Add water and shake to make the sulphur dioxide dissolve.

First you must burn the sulphur.

1 Copy and complete the word equation for this reaction.

   sulphur + _____ $\longrightarrow$ _____ _____

Then you must dissolve the sulphur dioxide in water.

2 How do you know that the solution is acidic?

You can make an **acidic** solution from carbon in exactly the same way.

3 Carbon dioxide makes a weaker acid than sulphur dioxide. How can you tell this from the diagram?

How nature makes nitric acid

Nitrogen doesn't burn in oxygen. But it will react with oxygen at the high temperature produced by a flash of lightning.

4 What substance is produced by the lightning?

5 What is produced when this gas dissolves in rain?

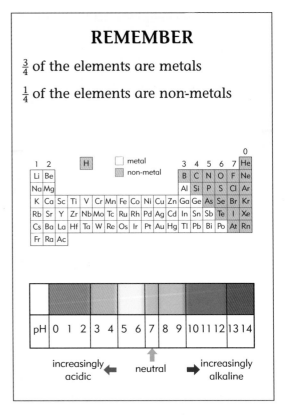

REMEMBER

$\frac{3}{4}$ of the elements are metals

$\frac{1}{4}$ of the elements are non-metals

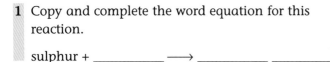

pH 0 1 2 3 4 5 6 7 8 9 10 11 12 13 14

increasingly acidic ← → neutral → increasingly alkaline

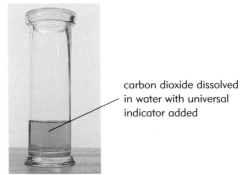

carbon dioxide dissolved in water with universal indicator added

Lightning makes thousands of tonnes of nitrogen oxides every year. These gases dissolve to make nitric acid.

These **oxides** all dissolve in water to make acids.

◼ Making an alkali from calcium

The diagrams show two ways of making an **alkaline** solution from a piece of calcium metal.

6 Copy and complete the word equations.

(a) calcium + water ⟶ ＿＿＿＿＿ + hydrogen

(b) calcium + oxygen ⟶ ＿＿＿＿＿ ＿＿＿＿＿

then

calcium oxide + water ⟶ ＿＿＿＿＿ ＿＿＿＿＿

Calcium hydroxide isn't very soluble. But some of it does dissolve to make an alkaline solution.

7 How do you know that the solution is alkaline?

oxygen   heated calcium   water

add water
and shake   calcium

calcium hydroxide
solution with universal
indicator added

◼ Making alkalis from other metals

Sodium and **potassium** hydroxide both dissolve in water. They produce alkaline solutions. Sodium and potassium both react with oxygen, and also with water, in the same way as calcium. But these reactions can be very dangerous.

8 Why do potassium and sodium react dangerously with water?

most reactive

potassium
sodium
calcium
magnesium

least reactive

What you need to remember [Copy and complete using the **key words**]

Making some acids and alkalis from elements

Non-metals such as sulphur, carbon and nitrogen react with oxygen to produce compounds called ＿＿＿＿＿＿＿＿.

These dissolve in water to make ＿＿＿＿＿＿＿＿ solutions.

If metal hydroxides dissolve in water, they make ＿＿＿＿＿＿＿＿ solutions.

Metals which have hydroxides that dissolve in water include ＿＿＿＿＿＿＿＿ and ＿＿＿＿＿＿＿＿.

Calcium hydroxide only partly dissolves in water.

1

Limestone – a useful rock

The ground under our feet is made of **rock** but you don't always see it. This is because the rock is often covered with soil. We also cover the ground with roads, pavements and buildings. If you dig down far enough you always reach solid rock. There are many different kinds of rock. One common rock is called limestone.

The diagram shows how we get limestone from the ground.

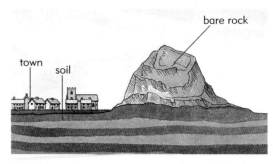

1 Copy and complete the following sentences.

We get limestone rock from places called _____ .

Large chunks of rock are blasted off using _____ .

We get limestone from **quarries**. Rock is blasted off the quarry face using explosives.

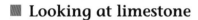
▥ Looking at limestone

The pictures show some pieces of limestone.

2 Describe carefully what each piece of limestone looks like.

Some types of limestone.

Chalk is a soft white limestone.

We cannot always tell if a piece of rock is limestone just by looking at it.

3 Look at the picture.

How can we test a rock to see if it really is limestone?

Drops of acid fizz when they are added to a lump of limestone.

Using limestone

Limestone is not a very hard rock so we can cut limestone into blocks and slabs quite easily. This makes limestone very useful for **buildings**. But there is a problem with using limestone for buildings as the picture shows.

4 Why is limestone a useful building material?

5 What is the problem when we use limestone for buildings?

6 Why is this problem worse today than it was hundreds of years ago?

Heating limestone

We don't use limestone just for building. We can also use limestone to make other useful materials. If we make limestone really hot we can change it into **quicklime**. We use a lime kiln to do this.

7 What is the waste gas released by heating limestone?

We can describe what happens in the lime kiln by writing a word equation for the reaction.

limestone + energy ⟶ quicklime + carbon dioxide

The chemical name for limestone is **calcium carbonate**.

The chemical name for quicklime is **calcium oxide**.

8 Write down the word equation using the chemical names.

Weather changes limestone. Acid rain makes it change even faster.

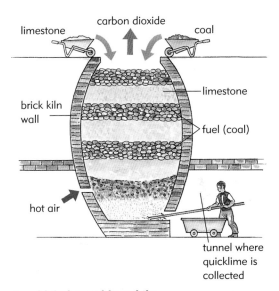

An old-fashioned lime kiln.

What you need to remember [Copy and complete using the **key words**]

Limestone – a useful rock

Limestone is a common _____. We get limestone from _____.

Limestone is very useful for _____ because it is easy to cut into blocks.

The chemical in limestone is _____ _____.

When we heat limestone strongly in a kiln it turns into _____.

The chemical name for quicklime is _____ _____.

What can we do with quicklime?

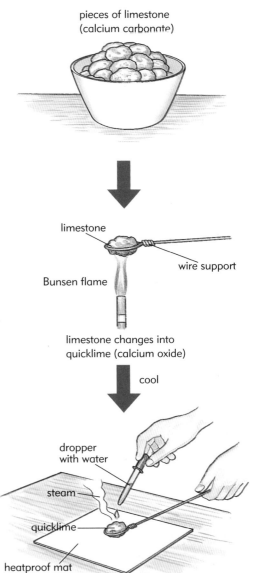

If you heat a piece of limestone strongly, it changes into a new material called quicklime. Quicklime looks almost the same as limestone, but when you add a few drops of water you can see the difference.

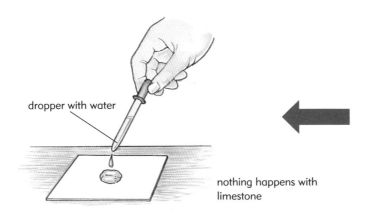

dropper with water

nothing happens with limestone

pieces of limestone (calcium carbonate)

limestone

wire support

Bunsen flame

limestone changes into quicklime (calcium oxide)

cool

dropper with water

steam

quicklime

heatproof mat

> **REMEMBER**
>
> Quicklime is calcium oxide.

1 What happens when you add a few drops of water to limestone?

2 What happens when you add a few drops of water to quicklime?

The quicklime **reacts** with the water to form a new material.

▥ What is the new material?

The new material formed from quicklime is called **slaked lime**.

3 Copy and complete the word equation.

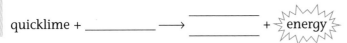

quicklime + _____ ⟶ _____ + energy

The chemical name for slaked lime is **calcium hydroxide**.

4 Write down the word equation using the chemical names for quicklime and slaked lime.

▥ What is so special about slaked lime?

Slaked lime dissolves just a little in water. We call this solution lime water.

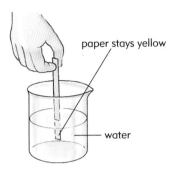

paper stays yellow

water

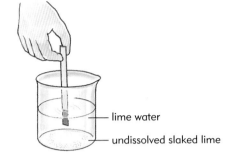

lime water

undissolved slaked lime

5 What happens when we test lime water with indicator paper?

6 What does this tell you about lime water?

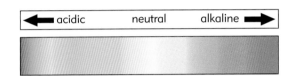

◀ acidic   neutral   alkaline ▶

▥ Using slaked lime

Soil in fields and gardens may become **acidic** if there is too much acid. If you add just the right amount of **alkali** to an acid soil, it makes it neutral. Most plants usually grow better when the soil is neutral.

Look at the photograph.

7 What is the farmer spreading on the field?

8 Write down <u>two</u> reasons why lime helps the soil.

9 Why must the farmer be careful not to add too much lime to the field?

Spreading lime. The lime neutralises soil acid. It also makes clay soil less sticky.

What you need to remember [Copy and complete using the **key words**]

What can we do with quicklime?

Quicklime _____ strongly with cold water. It forms a new material

called _____ _____.

This has the chemical name of _____ _____.

Slaked lime is an _____, it can neutralise acids.

Most plants do not grow well in acidic soils.

Farmers use slaked lime to make soils less _____.

3

Other useful materials made from limestone

Many of the things we build today are made from concrete. When wet concrete sets, it becomes as hard as stone. When we mix concrete it can be poured into moulds. This is how we make concrete into lots of different shapes.

1 Write down <u>two</u> things we can make using concrete.

2 Write down <u>two</u> reasons why concrete is useful for making these things.

To make concrete you need **cement**. Cement is made from limestone.

These objects were made using concrete.

▥ Making cement

We need to use two materials from the ground to make cement. These are the raw materials.

3 What <u>two</u> raw materials do you need to make cement?

4 What do you have to do to these raw materials to turn them into cement?

5 Write down <u>two</u> reasons why the kiln rotates all the time.

▥ Making concrete

The diagram shows how you can make **concrete**.

6 What <u>four</u> things must you mix together to make concrete?

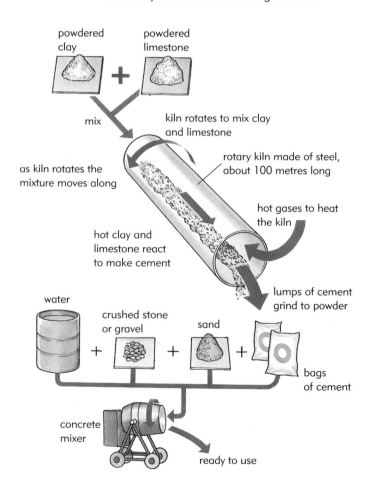

Earth materials

Using concrete

Once you have mixed some concrete you need to make it the right shape. The diagrams show how you can do this. The water **reacts** slowly with the cement to make the concrete set hard as stone. This can take a few days.

7 How can you keep the sides of the new concrete step straight?

8 Why should you wait a few days before removing the wooden frame?

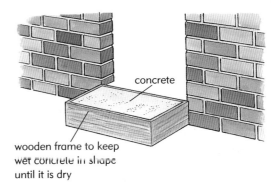

wooden frame to keep wet concrete in shape until it is dry

Making a concrete step for a house.

Making glass

Glass is another very useful material that we make using limestone.

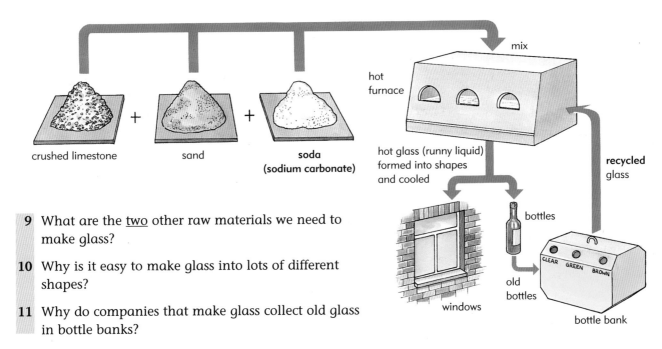

crushed limestone + sand + soda (sodium carbonate)

hot furnace

mix

hot glass (runny liquid) formed into shapes and cooled

recycled glass

bottles

windows

old bottles

bottle bank

9 What are the <u>two</u> other raw materials we need to make glass?

10 Why is it easy to make glass into lots of different shapes?

11 Why do companies that make glass collect old glass in bottle banks?

What you need to remember [Copy and complete using the **key words**]

Other useful materials made from limestone

We heat limestone and clay together in a hot kiln to make _____ .

A mixture of cement, sand, rock and water gives _____.

The water _____ with the cement and makes the concrete set solid.

Glass is a very useful material. You need to heat a mixture of limestone, sand and _____ to make glass.

Soda has the chemical name _____ _____.

We can melt old glass and use it again. We say that the glass has been _____.

Earth materials

4

Rocks made from hot liquid

The ground under our feet is usually made of soil with rock below it. This solid rock does not reach all the way to the centre of the Earth. The deeper underground you go, the hotter it gets. Before you get very many kilometres deep, it is hot enough to make rocks melt.

1 Copy and complete the following sentences.

The solid rock on the outside of the Earth is called the _____ . Below this is hot, sticky, partly molten rock called _____ .

Some of the rocks in the Earth's crust are made from magma that has cooled down. We can see this happen today when a volcano is active.

crust, solid rock, which is 10–90 kilometres thick

solid inner core

molten (liquid) outer core (6000 °C)

hot, sticky, molten rock called **magma**

▥ Why are there volcanoes?

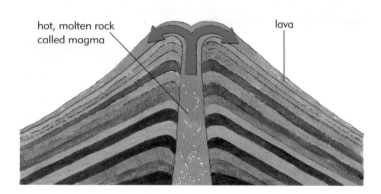

hot, molten rock called magma

lava

In some places the Earth's crust is thinner and weaker. Hot, molten rock from below can sometimes burst through the crust. This is how volcanoes start.

The molten rock soon cools down and turns solid. Rocks formed from molten magma are called **igneous** rocks. The word 'igneous' means 'formed by fire'.

2 Copy the flow diagram. Use the words <u>igneous rock</u>, <u>lava</u> and <u>magma</u> to complete it.

	volcano		cools down	
_____	→	_____	→	_____

3 (a) Write down the name of <u>one</u> igneous rock.

(b) Why are rocks like this called igneous rocks?

Lava is molten rock outside the Earth's crust. It cools quickly. A rock called basalt is often formed from the lava.

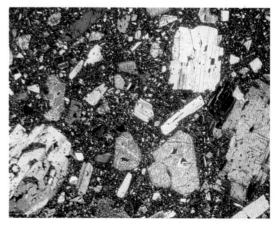

Basalt.

Earth materials

Two kinds of igneous rock

Basalt forms from molten rock that cools down quickly outside the Earth's crust. The diagram shows how another igneous rock forms. This rock is granite, and it forms from molten rock that cools down slowly inside the Earth's crust.

Basalt is called an **extrusive** igneous rock because it forms <u>outside</u> the Earth's crust.

Granite is called an **intrusive** igneous rock because it forms <u>inside</u> the Earth's crust.

4 Write down <u>two</u> differences in the ways that basalt and granite form.

5 Look at the pictures of thin slices of basalt and granite. Copy and complete the following sentences.

Basalt and granite both contain crystals. The crystals in granite are _____. This is because the magma cooled _____ and the crystals had time to grow.

Using granite

Granite is a very hard rock, so it does not wear away quickly. It looks good when it is polished.

6 Which picture shows clearly that granite does not wear away?

7 Write down <u>one</u> other use of granite that depends on the rock being hard wearing.

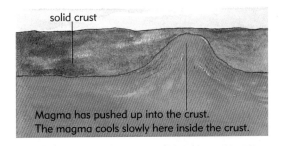

solid crust

Magma has pushed up into the crust.
The magma cools slowly here inside the crust.

Granite has **large** crystals.
Basalt has **small** crystals.

Rocks under the microscope.

Headstone made of limestone.
Headstone made of granite.

Sea wall made of granite.

What you need to remember [Copy and complete using the **key words**]

Rocks made from hot liquid

The Earth has a _____ of solid rock on the outside. Under this is hot, molten rock called _____.

Rocks that form when hot, molten rock cools down are called _____ rocks.

Magma that flows outside the crust is called _____. Basalt forms from lava that has cooled outside the crust, so we say it is an _____ igneous rock. Basalt cools quickly, so it contains _____ crystals.

Granite forms from magma that has cooled inside the crust. We say it is an _____ igneous rock. Granite cools slowly, so it contains _____ crystals.

5

Rocks made from bits of other rocks

Rocks at the Earth's surface slowly wear away. When rocks break up they leave lots of small bits of rock.

1 What breaks up the rock in this way?

2 Write down <u>two</u> things that can happen to the bits of rock.

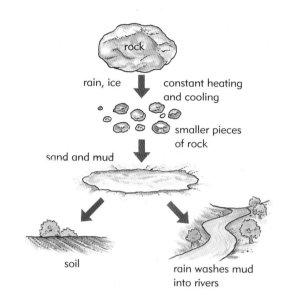

▥ What happens to mud and sand in rivers?

When water flows fast in a stream or river, it carries bits of **sand** and mud along with it. This is like stirring sand and water in a bucket.

3 Look at the diagrams. Then copy and complete the following sentences.

When you stop stirring, the sand _____ to the bottom of the bucket. We call the layers of sand a _____.

When a river reaches a lake or the sea, the water slows down.

When you stop stirring, the sand slowly falls to the bottom. We call this a **sediment**.

The sand is carried along with the water as you stir.

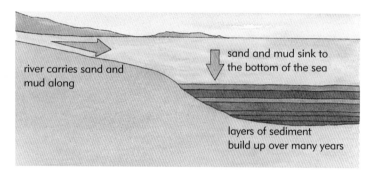

river carries sand and mud along

sand and mud sink to the bottom of the sea

layers of sediment build up over many years

4 When the river water stops flowing, what happens to the sand and mud it was carrying along?

▥ What happens to sediments in seas and lakes?

The diagram shows how the sediment at the bottom of the sea or lake slowly turns into hard rock. The new rocks are called **sedimentary** rocks. It can take millions of years for sedimentary rocks to form.

You need the information on the diagram to help answer question 5.

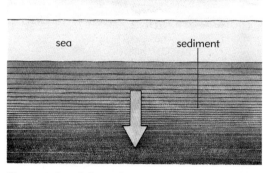

sea   sediment

The weight of the sediment layers presses down on the layers below. This squeezes out any water. Natural chemicals stick the bits of sand and mud together. We say they are **cemented**.

Earth materials

5 Read these sentences and then write them down in the right order. The first one has been done for you.

Rivers carry sand and mud to lakes and seas.

- Chemicals in the water cement the bits of sand and mud together.

- The bits of sand and mud fall to the bottom as a sediment.

- A new sedimentary rock has now formed.

- More and more layers of sediment pile up.

- The weight of all the layers squeezes out most of the water from the sediment.

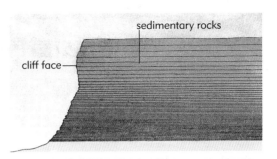

What do sedimentary rocks look like?

The picture shows a cliff and two pieces of rock found in it. You can tell that the cliff is made of sedimentary rock because you can see the layers.

6 (a) How are sandstone and mudstone similar to each other?

(b) How are they different?

Mudstone has very fine grains and a pattern of very thin bands.

Sandstone has bigger grains and a pattern of very thin bands.

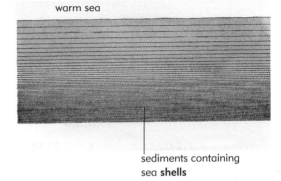

sediments containing sea **shells**

How limestone forms

Limestone is also a sedimentary rock.

7 What bits of material make up the sediment that forms limestone?

8 Limestone is mainly calcium carbonate. Explain why.

Sea shells contain **calcium carbonate**.

What you need to remember [Copy and complete using the **key words**]

Rocks made from bits of other rocks

Layers of _____ and mud pile up at the bottom of lakes and seas. These are called _____.

Over millions of years, the weight of the sediment squeezes out the water. Natural chemicals then stick the bits together, and we say that the bits have been _____. The rock that is formed is a kind of _____ rock.

Sandstone is a sedimentary rock made from bits of sand. Limestone contains bits of _____. This is why limestone is mainly made of the chemical _____ _____.

6

Which are the oldest rocks?

Nearly all rocks are very old compared to people. A rock that is 80 million years old is really quite young! Some rocks are much older than others.

1 Look at the diagrams. Copy and complete the following sentences.

The first layer of sediment is at the _____.

The last layer of sediment is at the _____.
This means that:

The oldest layer is at the _____.
The youngest layer of rock is at the _____.

▨ Rocks that have moved

Even if rocks have moved we can often tell which ones are the oldest.

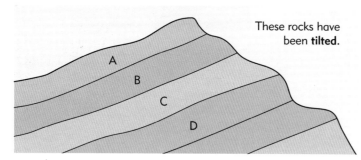

These rocks have been **tilted**.

2 Write down <u>three</u> different ways in which rocks can be moved.

3 Look at the rock layers A, B, C, D.

(a) Which is the youngest rock?

(b) Which is the oldest rock?

We can match the layers of rock that have been moved along a fault line or folded and partly worn away.

4 Find the rock on the right of the fault that is the same age as rock C.

5 Copy and complete the following sentences.

In the folded rocks:

Rock _____ is the same as rock A.

Rock _____ is the same as rock B.

REMEMBER

Sedimentary rocks are formed from layers of sediment containing sand, mud or shells.

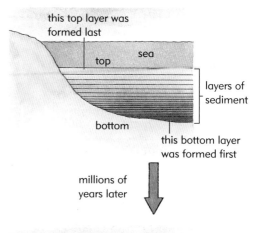

this top layer was formed last

sea

top

layers of sediment

bottom

this bottom layer was formed first

millions of years later

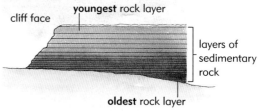

cliff face

youngest rock layer

layers of sedimentary rock

oldest rock layer

These rocks have fractured. They have broken and slipped. We say that they have been **faulted**.

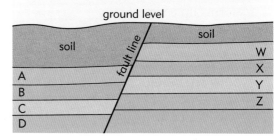

ground level

soil

soil

fault line

A

B

C

D

W

X

Y

Z

These rocks have been **folded**.
Then they have been partly worn away.

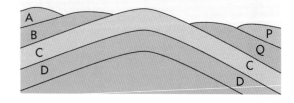

A

B

C

D

P

Q

C

D

Earth materials

Using fossils to tell the age of rocks

In sedimentary rocks we often find **fossils**. These are the remains of **plants** and **animals**. Fossils tell us which kinds of plants and animals lived when the sediments were formed. Rocks that contain the same kinds of fossils are probably about the same **age**.

6 (a) Which kinds of rock contain fossils?

(b) Why don't you find fossils in igneous rocks?

7 How old are the following rocks?

(a) Rocks that contain dinosaur bones.

(b) Rocks that contain trilobites but not crinoids.

(c) Rocks that contain both sharks and crinoids.

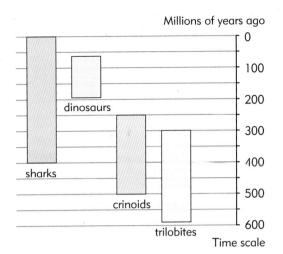

The bars show the ages of the fossils you might find.

Upside down rocks

Sometimes layers of sedimentary rocks can get turned **upside down** by Earth movements. We know this has happened because of the ages of the fossils in the rocks.

8 Look at the diagram.

A friend says that these are sedimentary rocks so the oldest rocks must be at the bottom. Do you agree? Give a reason for your answer.

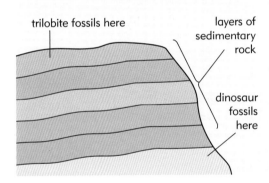

What you need to remember [Copy and complete using the **key words**]

Which are the oldest rocks?

With sedimentary rocks:

the layer of rock at the bottom is usually the _____,

the layer of rock at the top is usually the _____.

This is usually true even when rocks have been moved, for example _____,

_____ or _____.

It is not true if the rocks have been turned _____ _____.

Sedimentary rocks often contain the remains of _____ and

_____ that lived at the time the sediment was laid down.

We call these remains _____.

Rocks with the same fossils are probably the same _____.

7

Rocks that have changed

Rocks deep inside the Earth's crust may get squeezed very hard and become very hot. The high **pressure** and high **temperature** can change rocks into new kinds of rocks called **metamorphic** rocks.

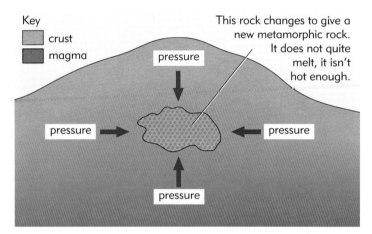

Key
- crust
- magma

This rock changes to give a new metamorphic rock. It does not quite melt, it isn't hot enough.

pressure

pressure

pressure

pressure

1 Copy and complete the following sentences.

When rocks change into metamorphic rocks, they become very hot but do not _____. If the rock did melt, it would cool to become an _____ rock.

Marble

Marble is a metamorphic rock. It has been changed from limestone.

Metamorphic rocks look different from the rocks that were changed. We say that they have a different **structure**. Metamorphic rocks feel different as well. We say that they have a different **texture**.

Look at the photographs.

2 Write down <u>two</u> differences between marble and limestone.

Look at the photograph of the rocks in acid.

3 Write down <u>two</u> ways in which marble and limestone are the same.

Limestone, a fairly soft rock that contains shells.

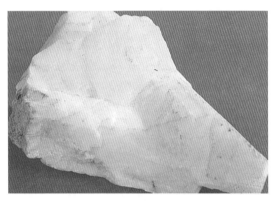

Marble, a hard rock made of crystals. Marble can be polished to give a shiny surface.

Both limestone and marble fizz when they are put in acids. Both rocks contain calcium carbonate.

Earth materials

■ Slate

Slate is a metamorphic rock. It has been changed from mudstone. Slate can be split with a chisel to give thin sheets.

4 (a) Write down <u>two</u> differences between slate and mudstone.

   (b) Why is slate a good material to use for the roof of a house?

Water soaks into mudstone.

Mudstone is a soft rock made from tiny bits of other rocks.

Slate is a hard rock. It splits into layers.

Thin sheets of slate are waterproof. We use them for roofs. They don't wear away.

■ Rocks with bands of crystals

Some metamorphic rocks contain bands of tiny **crystals**. Sometimes you can see the crystals without having to use a magnifying glass. The photographs show two rocks of this type.

5 (a) Write down the names of <u>two</u> metamorphic rocks that show bands of crystals.

   (b) What difference can you see between these two metamorphic rocks?

Schist

■ Rocks can be changed in other ways

High temperature and high pressure in the Earth's crust can do more than produce metamorphic rocks. They can also make new mountains. You can read about this on pages 64 to 65.

Gneiss

What you need to remember [Copy and complete using the **key words**]

Rocks that have changed

Deep inside the Earth's crust there can be high _____ and high _____. These can change rocks.

We call the changed rocks _____ rocks.

Limestone can be changed into _____, and mudstone can be changed into _____.

The changed rocks look different, they have a different _____.

The changed rocks also feel different, they have a different _____.

Some metamorphic rocks have bands of _____.

8

Identifying rocks

The previous few pages are all about rocks. These pages give you the chance to use many of the ideas you have learned about rocks.

Use the rock key on page 61 to answer questions 1 and 2.

1 A rock collector wrote some notes about a rock.

What was the rock?

2 The table shows notes that a student made at the same time as looking carefully at three rocks.

What were the rocks A, B and C?

The rock does not fizz at all with acid.

The particles in the rock (called the grains) are crystals arranged in layers.

The rock is hard but I can split it into sheets.

Rock	A	B	C
fizz with acid	no	no	yes
crystals	yes	no	no
crystals in layers	no	—	—
large crystals	yes	—	—
round grains	—	yes	no

■ Types of rock

The diagram shows how all the different types of rock are formed.

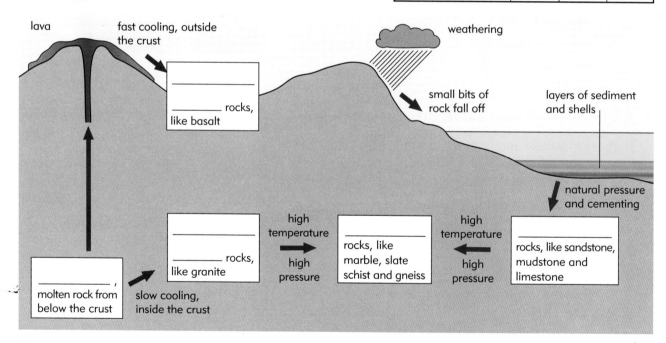

3 Copy the diagram.

Then add these words in the right places.

extrusive igneous   intrusive igneous

magma   metamorphic

sedimentary

Earth materials

4 Quartzite is a metamorphic rock. It is changed sandstone.

Copy and complete.

sandstone   high _____   ➡   quartzite
      high _____

Sandstone.

5 Write down these three headings.

   Igneous   Sedimentary   Metamorphic

Now write down the names of all the rocks in the key under the right headings.

6 What size grains do you find in these rocks?

(a) sandstone

(b) mudstone

Quartzite.

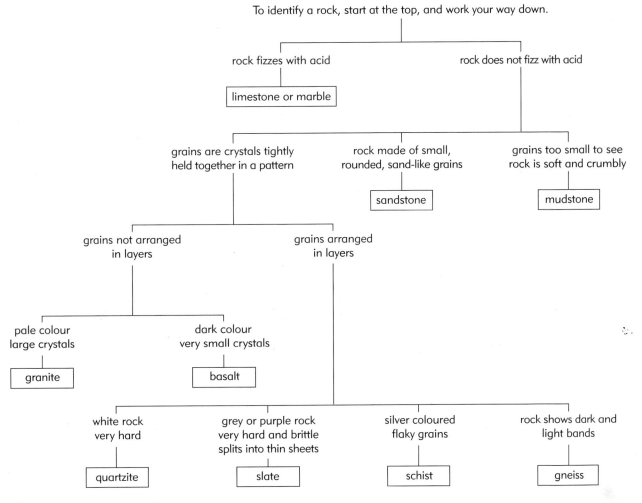

A key to some common rocks.

9

The Earth

The Earth is nearly **spherical**. This means that it is round like a ball, although it is not perfectly round.

Look at the pictures.

1 Write down <u>two</u> things that mean the Earth is not perfectly round.

■ Inside the Earth

Scientists think that the Earth is made of different layers inside. The diagram shows what these layers probably look like, but nobody has ever seen the layers. Even the deepest drill cannot make a hole right through the Earth's **crust**.

2 Imagine that you could drill a hole through the Earth to the centre.

Copy and complete the following sentences to say what you would find on the way through.

(a) First the drill would go through the solid rock in the Earth's _____.

(b) Next, on the outside of the mantle there would be sticky molten rock called _____.

(c) Deeper into the mantle the rock would be _____.

(d) About halfway through to the centre of the Earth the drill would reach the outer _____.

This is made of liquid _____ and _____ metals.

(e) The inner core is made of the same two metals but they are _____.

The Earth is much heavier than if it were only rock inside. We say that it has a higher density.

3 Why is the Earth much denser than rock?

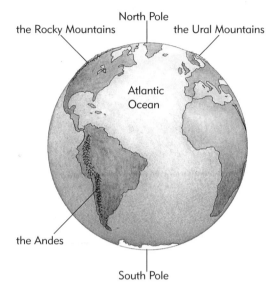

The surface of the Earth is bumpy. The Earth is slightly flattened at the North and South Poles.

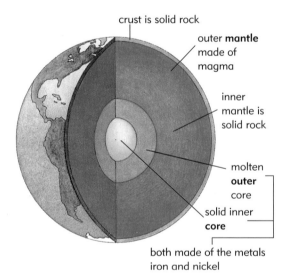

Magma is very thick and sticky molten rock. We say it is very **viscous**.
Nickel and **iron** are much heavier materials than rock. We say they are **denser** than rock.

Changes to the Earth's crust

The Earth's crust is changing all the time. Some of the changes happen quickly, but other changes are slow and can take millions of years. Look at the two diagrams and the two text boxes.

4 Write down <u>two</u> things that can change the Earth's crust quickly.

New rocks can form when things happen to the Earth's crust.

5 Copy the headings and complete the table.

What happens to the Earth's crust	Kind of rock formed

Some of the changes that happen to the Earth's crust wear away the hills and mountains. Other changes help to form new hills and mountains.

6 Write down <u>two</u> changes that help to make new mountains.

When new mountains are made, rocks can be pushed up thousands of metres. This needs huge forces.

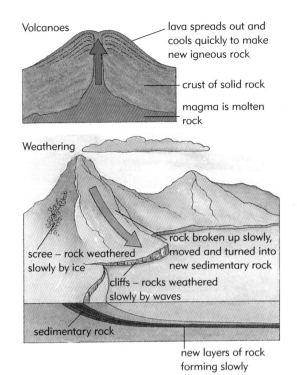

Volcanoes — lava spreads out and cools quickly to make new igneous rock

crust of solid rock

magma is molten rock

Weathering

scree – rock weathered slowly by ice

rock broken up slowly, moved and turned into new sedimentary rock

cliffs – rocks weathered slowly by waves

sedimentary rock

new layers of rock forming slowly

Earthquakes
The crust can move and break quickly in an earthquake.

Rocks folding
Large forces can make rocks fold slowly. When rocks are folded upwards, they can form new hills and mountains. Some rocks can be changed into metamorphic rocks.

What you need to remember [Copy and complete using the **key words**]

The Earth

The Earth is shaped like a ball. We say it is nearly _____.

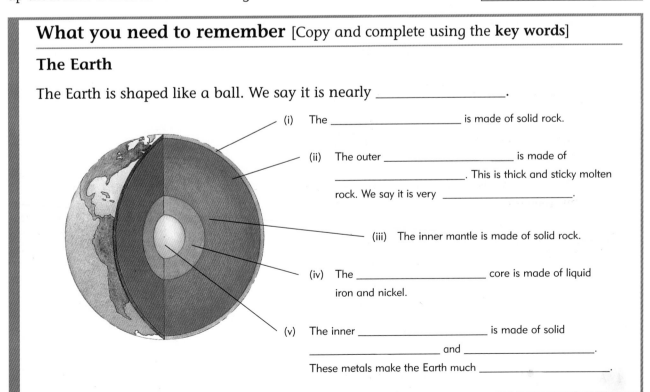

(i) The _____ is made of solid rock.

(ii) The outer _____ is made of _____. This is thick and sticky molten rock. We say it is very _____.

(iii) The inner mantle is made of solid rock.

(iv) The _____ core is made of liquid iron and nickel.

(v) The inner _____ is made of solid _____ and _____. These metals make the Earth much _____.

Earth materials

10

Movements that make mountains

Movements of the Earth's crust can push up rocks for thousands of metres. This forms new mountains. Rocks can move from the bottom of the sea to the top of a mountain.

1 How do we know that rocks can move this far?

The movements of the Earth's crust produce very large forces.

How can the Earth's crust move?

The diagram shows how the Earth's crust can move.

This fossil came from an animal that lived in the sea millions of years ago.

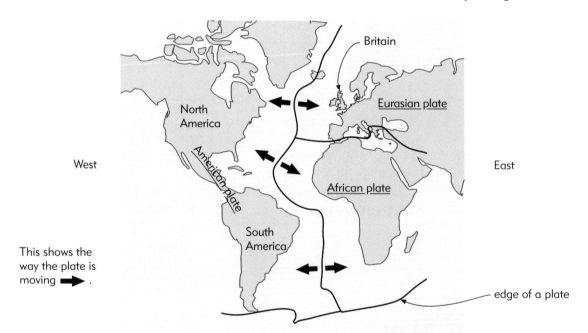

This shows the way the plate is moving ➡.

2 Copy and complete the following sentences.

Britain is on the _____ plate. North and South America are on the American _____.

3 (a) Which way is the American plate moving?

(b) Which way is the Eurasian plate moving?

(c) What is happening to the distance between America and Europe?

4 A plate moves about 5 cm each year. How far will the plate move in 1000 years?

The Earth's crust is not made of a single big piece. There are many large cracks in the Earth's crust. These cracks split the crust into very large pieces called **tectonic plates**. The plates **move** all the time. They do not move very fast, just a few **centimetres** (cm) each year. But these small movements add up to big movements over a long time.

Earth materials

The Earth today

The Earth millions of years ago

The **shapes** of South America and Africa fit together.

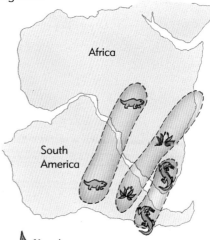

▥ How do we know that plates move?

South America and Africa are on different plates. These plates have been moving away from each other for millions of years. Long ago, South America and Africa must have been together. Look at the diagrams.

5 The shapes of South America and West Africa tell us that they were once together. Explain why.

6 The rocks in South America and Africa also tell us that they were once joined together. Explain why.

Fossils of this fern have been found all over Africa and South America.

Fossils of this reptile have been found in Brazil and in Africa.

Fossils of this reptile have been found in Argentina and in southern Africa.

▥ How moving plates can make new mountains

Some of the plates of the Earth's crust are moving away from each other. Other plates are pushing into each other. When two plates move towards each other they can force rocks upwards to give new **mountains**.

7 Look at the diagram.

(a) Which <u>two</u> plates are pushing into each other?

(b) Which mountains have been formed by these moving plates?

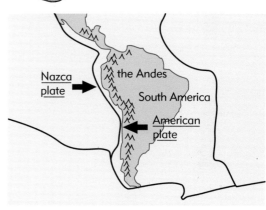

What you need to remember [Copy and complete using the **key words**]

Movements that make mountains

The Earth's crust is cracked into large pieces. We call these _____ _____.

The plates _____ very slowly, just a few _____ each year.

Millions of years ago, South America and Africa were next to each other. We know this because:

■ their _____ fit together well

■ they have rocks containing the same _____.

In some places, tectonic plates push together. This forces some rocks upwards and makes new _____.

Earth materials

11

What keeps the Earth's crust moving?

Below the Earth's crust is hot molten rock called **magma**. When there are movements in the magma, the crust floating on top moves as well.

What makes liquids move?

If a liquid gets hot, it moves around. The diagrams show what happens.

1 Copy and complete the following sentences.

Water _____ around when you heat it. This is because hot water _____ and cold water moves _____ to take its place.

These movements are called **convection** currents.

> ## REMEMBER
> The Earth's crust is cracked into pieces called tectonic plates. These plates move around slowly.

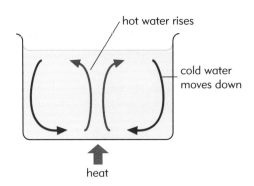

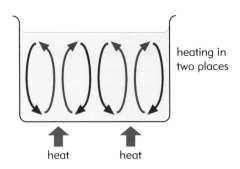

Convection currents inside the Earth

Heat produced inside the Earth causes slow convection currents in the magma.

Look at the diagram.

2 Copy and complete the following sentences.

Convection currents in the magma.

■ make plates A and B move _____

■ make plates B and C move _____.

The plates can move because they _____ on top of the magma. The moving magma can make the plates move because it is very _____.

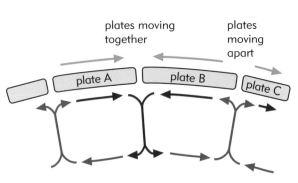

The tectonic plates float on the magma. Hot magma is a very thick, sticky liquid. We say it is viscous.

Earth materials

How does the inside of the Earth keep hot?

Something must be heating up the magma or there wouldn't be any convection currents.

Radioactive substances inside the Earth produce the heat that is needed. The diagram shows how they do this.

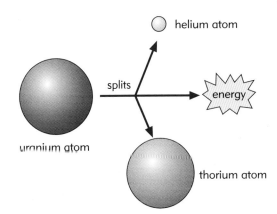

3 Copy and complete the following sentences.

Uranium atoms _____ up into smaller atoms of _____ and _____. This change also releases some _____.

4 Radioactive substances will keep on heating up the inside of the Earth for a long time to come. Explain why.

The Earth formed about 4.5 billion (4 500 000 000) years ago. Since then, about half of the uranium atoms have split up.

What happens when the tectonic plates move apart

When tectonic plates push against each other, new mountains form.

The diagram shows what happens when plates move apart.

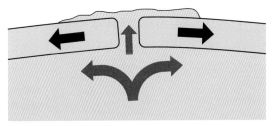

When two plates move apart, magma fills the gap. The magma quickly cools to form the igneous rock called basalt.

5 (a) What type of new rock spreads out through the cracks between plates?

(b) Why is this type of rock formed?

6 Look at the map. Write down the name of a country where basalt is forming.

The edges of the plates that are moving apart are usually under the sea.

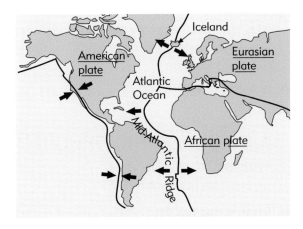

What you need to remember [Copy and complete using the **key words**]

What keeps the Earth's crust moving?

Tectonic plates move because of _____ currents in the _____ below the Earth's crust.
The energy that produces the currents comes from _____ substances inside the Earth.

Earth materials

12 Changing ideas about the Earth

Until about two hundred years ago, most people believed that the mountains, valleys and seas on the Earth had always been just like they are today. Many of these people thought the Earth was created only a few thousand years ago.

Then geologists started to study the rocks and to think about how they were formed. They realised that the Earth must be many millions of years old.

1 Why did they think that the Earth must be millions of years old?

2 What else did they then need to explain?

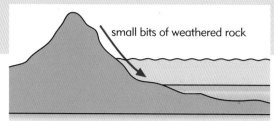
small bits of weathered rock

Thick layers of sedimentary rock must take millions of years to form.

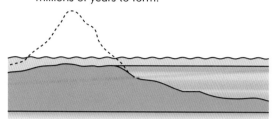

Mountains would be completely worn away over millions of years. So geologists need to explain how new mountains are formed.

A cooling, shrinking Earth

The diagrams show one theory about how new mountains are formed.

3 Write down the following sentences in the correct order.

■ The molten core carries on cooling, but more and more slowly. It shrinks as it cools.

■ The Earth began as a ball of hot, molten rock.

■ The shrinking core makes the crust wrinkle. The high places become mountains, the low places become seas.

■ As the molten rock cooled, a solid crust formed.

According to this theory, the Earth can't be more than about 400 million years old or it would be completely solid by now.

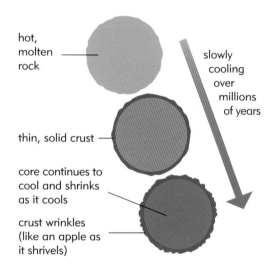
hot, molten rock

slowly cooling over millions of years

thin, solid crust

core continues to cool and shrinks as it cools

crust wrinkles (like an apple as it shrivels)

Problems for the shrinking Earth theory

We now know that the Earth contains quite a lot of radioactive elements such as uranium. The atoms of these elements gradually decay (break up). Heat is released as they do so.

4 What effect does this have on the Earth's core?

5 The oldest rocks scientists have found on Earth are more than 3.5 billion years old. How do scientists know this?

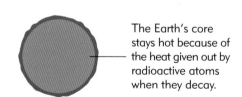
The Earth's core stays hot because of the heat given out by radioactive atoms when they decay.

Dating rocks
Scientists can measure
■ the amounts of radioactive atoms in rocks
■ the amounts of atoms produced when the radioactive atoms decay.
This tells them how old the rocks are.

Earth materials

▨ The idea of a moving crust

We think that mountains are formed by the Earth's crust moving about. Some scientists first suggested this idea nearly 150 years ago but most scientists didn't agree.

6 Why did some scientists suggest that the Earth's crust is moving?

7 Why did other scientists not agree?

During the 1950s, scientists started to explore the rocks at the bottom of the oceans. The diagrams show what they found and how they explained it.

8 Copy and complete the following sentences.

Under the oceans are long _____ ridges.

These are made of rock that is quite _____.

The sea floor under the ocean is moving _____.

Magma from below the Earth's _____ moves up to make new rock.

The Earth's crust is made of a small number of separate sections called plates. Under the oceans these plates are moving apart. But in some places these plates are moving towards each other. This pushes rock upwards to make new mountains.

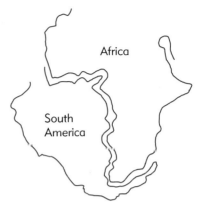

Some scientists suggested that South America and Africa must once have been together. Other scientists said that there was no way they could possibly have moved apart.

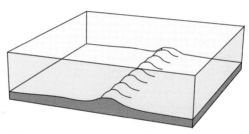

There are long mountain ridges underneath the ocean. They are made of young rocks.

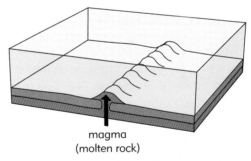

magma
(molten rock)

Sections of crust on the sea floor are moving apart. New rock forms to fill the gap.

What you need to remember

Changing ideas about the Earth

You should be able to:
- ▪ describe the 'shrinking Earth' model of how mountains are formed;
- ▪ explain why this model has been replaced by the idea of the Earth's crust being made up of moving plates.

13

Where does oil come from?

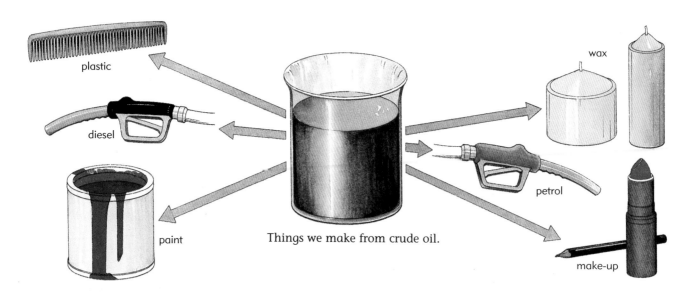

Things we make from crude oil.

We find many useful substances in the Earth's **crust**. One of these substances is oil. We call the oil that comes out of the ground **crude** oil.

1 Write down some of the things that we can make from crude oil.

How did the crude oil get there?

Crude oil was made many **millions** of years ago. The sea was full of tiny animals. When these animals died they piled up on the sea bed. The diagrams show how these dead animals changed into oil.

2 Put these sentences into the right order to explain how oil was made. The first sentence has been put in place for you.

Millions of tiny animals lived in the seas.

■ The pressure and heat of the rocks turned the dead animals into oil.

■ As the dead animals decayed they were covered with layers of mud.

■ When the animals died their bodies fell to the bottom of the sea.

■ The layers of mud slowly changed into layers of rock.

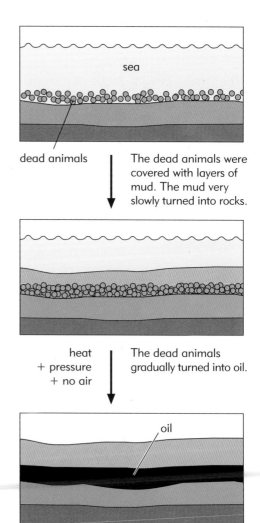

sea

dead animals — The dead animals were covered with layers of mud. The mud very slowly turned into rocks.

heat + pressure + no air — The dead animals gradually turned into oil.

oil

How do we get oil from the ground?

Oil forms in small drops which are spread through lots and lots of rock. Luckily for us, the oil doesn't stay like this. A lot of oil often collects together in one place, as you can see in the diagrams.

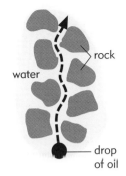

water → rock

drop of oil

Many rocks have lots of tiny spaces. Oil and water can move through these spaces. We say the rocks are **permeable**. Oil **floats** on water. So oil rises to the top of the permeable rocks.

3 Copy and complete the following sentences.

Oil rises up through _____ rock because it floats on _____.

It collects underneath a layer of _____ rock.

4 What must you do to collect the trapped oil?

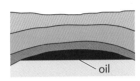

oil

When the oil reaches an impermeable layer it can't rise any further. The oil is **trapped** under the rock. (Impermeable means <u>not</u> permeable.)

What are fossil fuels?

Fossils, like oil, come from the remains of plants and animals from millions of years ago. We can collect some of these very old remains and use them as fuels, which we call **fossil** fuels.

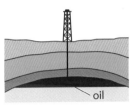

oil

To get the oil you have to **drill** down through the impermeable layer.

coal

fossil fuels

oil

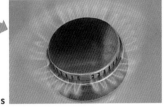

natural gas

5 Write down the names of <u>two</u> useful fuels we get from crude oil.

6 Write down the names of <u>two</u> other fossil fuels.

What you need to remember [Copy and complete using the **key words**]

Where does oil come from?

We find oil in the Earth's _____. This is called _____ oil.

Oil was made from things that lived in the sea _____ of years ago.

Fuels that are made from dead plants or animals are called _____ fuels.

Two other fossil fuels are _____ and _____ _____.

Oil _____ on water so it rises up through _____ rocks.

When the oil reaches an impermeable rock it becomes _____.

To get this oil we need to _____ down through the layers of impermeable rock.

Earth materials

14

Oil – what would we do without it?

Crude oil contains many useful **fuels**. It also contains many other chemicals that we can use to make new **materials**, like plastics.

1 Which substance from crude oil does the car use as a fuel?

2 Use the diagram to help you copy and complete this table. The first row is filled in for you.

Part of car	Substance made from crude oil
tyres	synthetic rubber
in engine	
bodywork	
steering wheel	
seat covers	
in fuel tank	

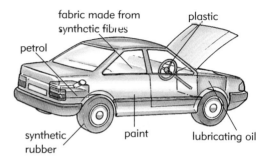

fabric made from synthetic fibres

plastic

petrol

synthetic rubber

paint

lubricating oil

We can make useful materials from crude oil. 'Synthetic' means made from chemicals not from parts of plants or animals.

▨ Making crude oil useful

When the crude oil comes out of the ground it isn't much use. We can't use it as a fuel or to make new materials. Crude oil is a **mixture** of lots of different things. We have to separate it into different parts before we can use it.

3 Use the information in the table to help you complete these sentences.

(a) Many of the substances in crude oil are used as fuels, for example _____, _____ and _____.

(b) The part of crude oil that is used for road making is called _____.

(c) Plastics are made from a part of crude oil called _____.

(d) Lubricating oil is used to reduce _____ between moving parts of _____.

Crude oil – a thick black liquid, a mixture of many things.

Part of crude oil	What it is used for
petrol	fuel for cars
naphtha	making plastics
kerosene	fuel for jets
diesel	fuel for lorries and factories
lubricating oil	reduces friction between moving parts of machines
bitumen	surfacing roads

How we use crude oil

The pie chart shows how much crude oil we use for different things.

4 (a) What is most crude oil used for?

(b) What percentage of oil is turned into plastics?

(c) Give <u>three</u> examples of things that use the energy stored in crude oil.

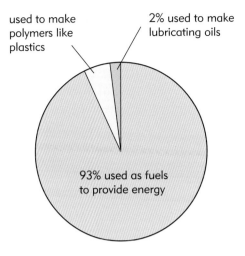

How we use crude oil.

How long will the oil last?

Oil and the other fossil fuels that we use today were formed millions of years ago.

Once we have used them up there won't be any more for millions of years.

The bar chart shows how long fossil fuels will last if we keep on using them at the present rate.

5 Copy the table.

Fossil fuel	Number of years until it runs out
oil	
natural gas	
coal	

Then use the bar chart to help you complete the table.

We will have problems when the oil runs out because we use it for so many things.

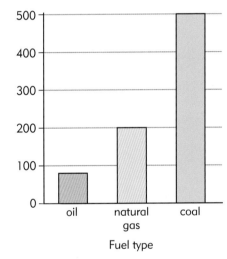

What you need to remember [Copy and complete using the **key words**]

Oil – what would we do without it?

Crude oil is a _____ of many different substances.

Some parts of the oil can be burned as _____.

We can also use the chemicals in oil to make new _____.

Earth materials

15

How crude oil is split up into parts

Crude oil is a mixture of lots of different liquids. These liquids are very useful, but we can't use them until we have separated them from each other.

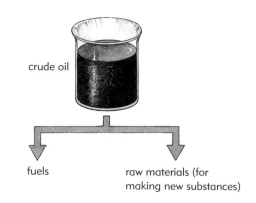

crude oil

fuels   raw materials (for making new substances)

1 Write down the <u>two</u> main uses for the liquids in crude oil.

◼ How to separate a mixture of liquids

If you heat up a liquid it changes to a vapour. We say it **evaporates**. If you make the liquid hot enough, it boils. A boiling liquid evaporates very quickly.

If you cool a vapour it changes back into a liquid. We say it **condenses**.

2 Copy the diagram on the right. Then complete it.

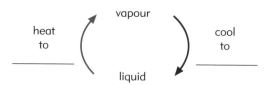

heat to ____   vapour   cool to ____

liquid

Evaporating a liquid and then condensing it again is called **distillation**.

We can use this idea to separate a mixture of liquids.

The diagram shows how brandy is made from wine.

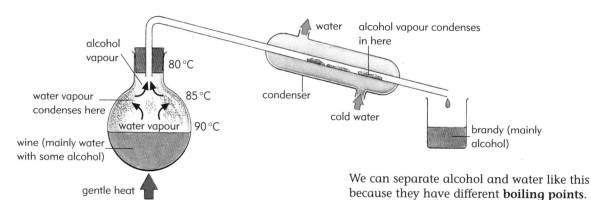

alcohol vapour   80 °C

water vapour condenses here   85 °C

water vapour   90 °C

wine (mainly water with some alcohol)

gentle heat

water   alcohol vapour condenses in here

condenser

cold water

brandy (mainly alcohol)

We can separate alcohol and water like this because they have different **boiling points**. Water boils at 100 °C, alcohol boils at 78 °C.

3 Copy and complete the following sentences.

The wine contains two liquids called _____ and _____.

The liquid alcohol boils at _____.

It turns into alcohol _____.

Droplets of alcohol form in the _____.

Water boils at _____.

Any water vapour _____ in the neck of the flask.

Separating a mixture of liquids into parts or fractions like this is called **fractional distillation**.

Earth materials

Separating crude oil into fractions

We use fractional distillation to separate crude oil into different parts or fractions. The different fractions boil at different temperatures.

Fraction of crude oil	Boiling points in °C
dissolved gases	below 0
petrol	around 65
naphtha	around 130
kerosene	around 200
diesel oil	around 300
bitumen	over 400

4 (a) Which fraction of crude oil has the highest boiling point?

(b) Which fraction has the lowest boiling point?

5 Explain why crude oil can be separated by fractional distillation.

6 Why is separating crude oil into fractions more difficult than making brandy?

An oil fractionating tower

In Britain, 250 000 tonnes of oil are produced every day! To separate all of this oil into its fractions we use enormous **fractionating towers**. The diagram shows one of these.

7 Copy and complete the following sentences.

Crude oil is heated to about _____ °C.

Bitumen has a _____ boiling point so it falls straight to the bottom of the tower.

Methane has a _____ boiling point so it goes straight to the top of the tower.

Fractions with in-between boiling points _____ partway up the tower.

The lower the boiling point of a fraction, the _____ it goes up the tower before it condenses.

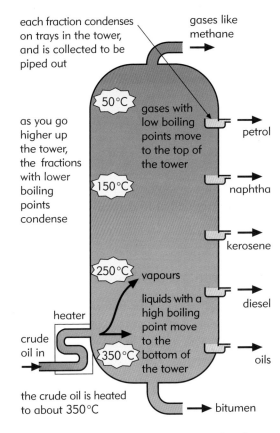

each fraction condenses on trays in the tower, and is collected to be piped out

gases like methane

as you go higher up the tower, the fractions with lower boiling points condense

50°C — gases with low boiling points move to the top of the tower

petrol

150°C

naphtha

kerosene

250°C — vapours

liquids with a high boiling point move to the bottom of the tower

diesel

heater

crude oil in

350°C

oils

the crude oil is heated to about 350°C

bitumen

A fractionating tower to separate crude oil.

What you need to remember [Copy and complete using the **key words**]

How crude oil is split up into parts

When you heat a liquid it _____ to form a vapour.

When you cool a vapour it _____ to form a liquid.

Evaporating a liquid and then condensing it again is called _____.

Separating a mixture of liquids like this is called _____ _____.

The liquids in the mixture must have different _____ _____.

Crude oil is separated into fractions in _____ _____.

16

What are the chemicals in crude oil?

In nature, there are about 90 different kinds of atom, which we call the elements. Substances that contain more than one kind of atom joined together are called **compounds**. Most of the substances in crude oil are compounds that are made from just two kinds of atom. The smallest part of each compound is a **molecule**. The diagram shows two of the molecules you find in crude oil.

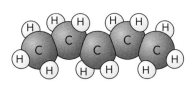

This molecule has 5 carbon atoms and 12 hydrogen atoms. We write this C_5H_{12}. This is the formula of the compound.

Key		carbon atom		hydrogen atom

1 Which <u>two</u> kinds of atom do these molecules contain?

2 What is the difference between the two molecules?

3 Write down the formula of

   (a) the smaller molecule

   (b) the larger molecule.

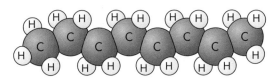

This molecule has 8 carbon atoms and 18 hydrogen atoms.

Molecules made only of **hydrogen** atoms and **carbon** atoms are called **hydrocarbons**. Most of the molecules in crude oil are hydrocarbons.

▌ Differences between hydrocarbons

Crude oil is a mixture of many different hydrocarbons. The hydrocarbon molecules are all different sizes and masses. The boiling point of a molecule depends on its size and mass. This means that the hydrocarbon molecules all boil at different temperatures.

4 Copy and complete the table.

Hydrocarbon	Formula	Boiling point in °C
butane		
hexane		
decane		

5 Copy and complete the following sentence.

The hydrocarbon with the biggest molecules boils at the _____ temperature.

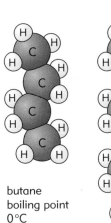

butane
boiling point
0°C

hexane
boiling point
70°C

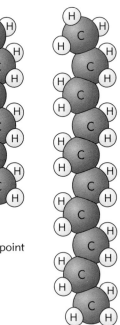

decane
boiling point
175°C

Earth materials

Which hydrocarbons are in which fractions?

Hydrocarbons with the **largest** molecules have the highest boiling points. These large molecules condense to liquids lower down the fractionating tower.

6 Which fraction of crude oil has the smallest molecules?

7 Which fraction of crude oil has the largest molecules?

8 Copy and complete the following sentences.

Diesel fuel has _____ molecules than kerosene.
Naphtha has _____ molecules than kerosene.

A simple way to say how big hydrocarbon molecules are is to count how many carbon atoms they have. The diagram below shows the hydrocarbons in some of the oil fractions.

9 How many carbon atoms are there in:

(a) the hydrocarbon molecules in petrol?

(b) the hydrocarbon molecules in diesel?

(c) the hydrocarbon molecules in bitumen?

10 How many carbon atoms would you expect to find in the hydrocarbon gases?

The crude oil fractions are different in more ways than their different boiling points. This is why we can use them for different jobs.

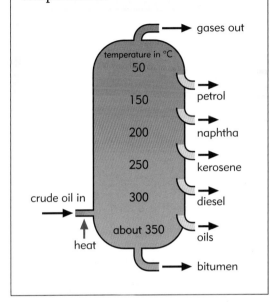

REMEMBER

The different fractions in crude oil condense to liquids at different temperatures.

temperature in °C	
	gases out
50	
150	petrol
200	naphtha
250	kerosene
300	diesel
about 350	oils
	bitumen

crude oil in — heat

Number of carbon atoms in a molecule

petrol   diesel   bitumen

1 2 3 4 5 6 7 8 9 10 11 12 13 14 15 16 17 18 19 20 21 22 23 24 25 26 27 28 29 30 31 32 33 34 35 36 37 38 39 40 41 42 43 44 45 46 47 48 49 50 51 52 53 54 55

What you need to remember [Copy and complete using the **key words**]

What are the chemicals in crude oil?

Substances that contain more than one kind of atom are called _____.

Most of the compounds in crude oil are made from two kinds of atoms. These are _____ atoms and _____ atoms. We call these compounds _____.

The smallest part of each hydrocarbon is called a _____.
Hydrocarbons with the highest boiling points have the _____ molecules.

Earth materials

17

Different hydrocarbons for different jobs

Different hydrocarbons have molecules of different sizes. This gives them different **properties**. One example is boiling points. Hydrocarbons with smaller molecules have lower boiling points. The properties of different hydrocarbons make them useful for different jobs.

> ### REMEMBER
>
> The compounds in crude oil contain hydrogen and carbon atoms. They are hydrocarbons.

Oil fraction	petrol	diesel	lubricating oil	bitumen
Number of carbon atoms	5 to 12	15 to 25	26 to 50	more than 50
Size of the molecules	small	fairly small	big	very big
Boiling point	low	fairly low	fairly high	high
Appearance				
A few drops left in the open air.	Quickly changes to a vapour. We say it is very **volatile**.	Slowly changes to vapour.	Very slowly changes to vapour.	Hardly changes to vapour at all.
A few drops soaked into glass wool.	Catches fire very easily. We say it is very **flammable**.	Catches fire quite easily.	Hard to light.	Hard to light.
How easy is it to pour?	Easy to pour.	Easy to pour.	Not easy to pour, it sticks to the sides.	Almost solid, very slow to pour. We say it is **viscous**.

1 Petrol and diesel are both used as fuels in engines. Which properties make them useful for this job? Give reasons for your answers.

2 Lubricating oil is used to make engines run smoothly. The oil reduces friction between moving parts. Which properties make it useful for this job? Explain why.

3 Bitumen is used to make the tarmac on roads. Which properties make it useful for this job? Give reasons for your answer.

▮ Making long hydrocarbons more useful

The longer hydrocarbon molecules in crude oil do not make very good **fuels**.

4 Write down <u>two</u> reasons why long hydrocarbon molecules do not make good fuels.

Earth materials

We can make long hydrocarbon molecules more useful if we split them up into smaller molecules. We call this **cracking**.

5 Copy and complete the word equation

$$decane \xrightarrow{\text{cracking}} \underline{\qquad} + \underline{\qquad}$$

$\left(\begin{array}{ccc} \text{10 carbon} & \underline{\quad}\text{ carbon} & \underline{\quad}\text{ carbon} \\ \text{atoms} & \text{atoms} & \text{atoms} \end{array}\right)$

A simpler way to write down this chemical reaction is to use the formula of each compound.

6 Copy and complete the formula equation

$$C_{10}H_{22} \xrightarrow{\text{cracking}} \underline{\qquad} + \underline{\qquad}$$

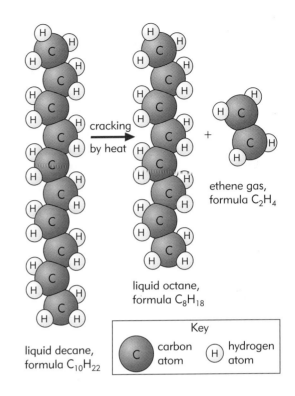

liquid decane, formula $C_{10}H_{22}$

ethene gas, formula C_2H_4

liquid octane, formula C_8H_{18}

Key		
C	carbon atom	H hydrogen atom

How we use the cracked hydrocarbons

Some of the smaller molecules made by cracking are useful as fuels. Octane is used in petrol. Other molecules can be used to make new materials such as plastics.

We use ethene to make the plastic polythene.

7 Why is octane better than decane for petrol?

Cracking a hydrocarbon at school

The diagram shows how you can crack a hydrocarbon.

8 Which <u>two</u> things show that you have cracked some of the liquid paraffin?

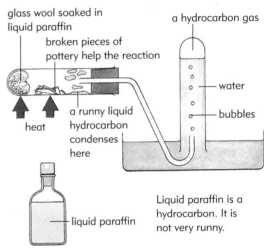

glass wool soaked in liquid paraffin

broken pieces of pottery help the reaction

a hydrocarbon gas

water

bubbles

a runny liquid hydrocarbon condenses here

heat

liquid paraffin

Liquid paraffin is a hydrocarbon. It is not very runny.

What you need to remember [Copy and complete using the **key words**]

Different hydrocarbons for different jobs

Small hydrocarbon molecules can:

evaporate quickly (we say they are very _____)

catch fire easily (we say they are very _____)

pour easily (we say they are not very _____)

Larger hydrocarbons do not have these _____ and so they are not very

good _____.

Large hydrocarbon molecules can be split up into smaller molecules that are more

useful. We call this _____.

18

Plastics from oil

We can crack long hydrocarbon molecules to give smaller molecules. Some of the smaller molecules are good fuels. Other molecules are useful to make new materials such as plastics.

Using ethene to make a plastic

One of the small molecules we get by cracking hydrocarbon molecules is called ethene. If we **join** many ethene molecules together, we get a very **long** molecule that is a useful plastic.

1 (a) What is the name of the plastic made from ethene?

(b) Why does the plastic have this name?

We usually call this plastic **polythene**.

What do we use polythene for?

The pictures show some of the things we can make using polythene. The box shows some of the properties of polythene.

> **Some properties of polythene**
>
> It is soft – you can scratch it easily and it wears away.
>
> It is tough – even if you drop it, it doesn't break.
>
> It isn't very clear – you cannot see clearly through it unless it is very thin.
>
> It is strong – it is hard to tear.
>
> It is flexible – you can bend it easily.
>
> It melts easily – but can stand boiling water.
>
> It is waterproof – liquids cannot soak through it.

2 Why wouldn't we use polythene to make these things?

(a) saucepans   (b) shoes   (c) car windscreen

PVC – another useful plastic

We can also make things from a plastic called **PVC**. This is short for **poly(vinyl chloride)**.

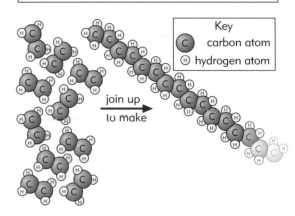

Key
C carbon atom
H hydrogen atom

join up to make

Lots of small ethene molecules join together to give a long molecule of poly(ethene). 'Poly' means 'many'.

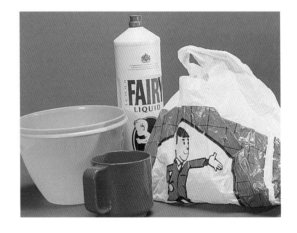

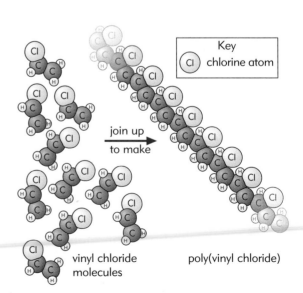

Key
Cl chlorine atom

join up to make

vinyl chloride molecules   poly(vinyl chloride)

Earth materials

3 Copy and complete the following sentence.

You need to join up lots of molecules of _____ _____ to make PVC.

All plastics are made by joining together lots of smaller molecules. We say that plastics are **polymers**.

PVC hosepipe.

Why is PVC useful?

PVC is waterproof, clear and colourless. It is stiff, so it does not bend easily. You can change PVC by adding other things to it. You can make it opaque so you cannot see through it and you can colour it. You can even make it flexible so that it bends easily.

The pictures show some things you can make using PVC.

4 For each object, write down <u>two</u> properties of PVC that make it a good material to use.

PVC window frame.

Comparing polythene and PVC

The box tells you about polythene and PVC.

5 Write down <u>two</u> ways in which polythene and PVC are the same.

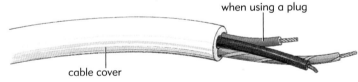

the colours are important when using a plug

cable cover

If there is an electrical fault, the wires can get hot.

6 Look at the diagram. Write down <u>two</u> reasons why PVC is better than polythene to make the covering for electrical cables.

> Polythene and PVC both melt easily. You can mould them into different shapes.
>
> Polythene and PVC are both insulators. Electricity cannot pass through them.
>
> Polythene can catch fire quite easily. PVC does not.
>
> PVC can be made in bright colours. The colours are not so good for polythene.

What you need to remember [Copy and complete using the **key words**]

Plastics from oils

Plastics have very _____ molecules. To make plastics we need to _____ together lots of small molecules.

The word 'poly' means many, so we say that plastics are _____.

Two common plastics are _____ and _____.

[You need to know some of the uses of PVC and polythene and why they are useful for these jobs.]

19

Burning fuels – where do they go?

We get gases, petrol and diesel from crude oil. When we burn these fuels, energy is released. New substances are also produced.

Look at the diagram.

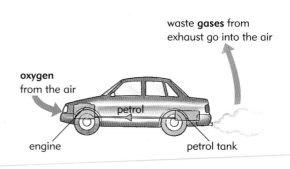

oxygen from the air

waste **gases** from exhaust go into the air

petrol

engine

petrol tank

1 What reacts with petrol to make it burn?

2 What happens to the new substances that are produced?

3 Copy and complete the word equation.

petrol + _____ ⟶ waste gases + energy

All the fuels we get from crude oil produce the same new substances when they burn.

▨ What new substances are made when fuels burn?

To find out what new substances are made when fuels burn, you need to trap them.

The diagram shows how you can do this.

4 What two substances are made when methane burns?

5 Copy and complete the word equation

methane _____

   + ⟶ _____ + _____ + energy

oxygen _____

6 Write down three different ways of showing that the droplets of liquid are water.

7 How can you tell that the gas produced is carbon dioxide?

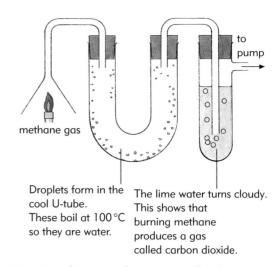

methane gas

to pump

Droplets form in the cool U-tube. These boil at 100 °C so they are water.

The lime water turns cloudy. This shows that burning methane produces a gas called carbon dioxide.

Trapping the new substances made when methane burns.

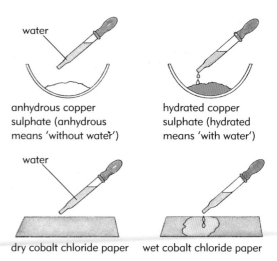

water

anhydrous copper sulphate (anhydrous means 'without water')

hydrated copper sulphate (hydrated means 'with water')

water

dry cobalt chloride paper

wet cobalt chloride paper

Two more tests for water.

Earth materials

What happens to molecules when methane burns?

The diagram shows what happens to a methane molecule when it burns.

8 Copy and complete the following sentences.

When methane burns

- the carbon atoms join with _____ atoms to make a molecule of _____ _____

- the hydrogen atoms join with _____ atoms to make a molecule of _____.

When anything burns, its atoms join with oxygen atoms to make **oxides**. Water is hydrogen oxide.

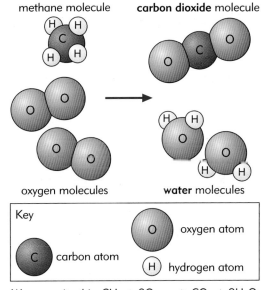

methane molecule   **carbon dioxide** molecule

oxygen molecules   **water** molecules

Key

O   oxygen atom

C   carbon atom

H   hydrogen atom

We can write this: $CH_4 + 2O_2 \longrightarrow CO_2 + 2H_2O$

Burning other fuels

Fuels from crude oil are all hydrocarbons. The diagrams show some hydrocarbon molecules.

9 Burning hydrocarbons always makes water and carbon dioxide. Why is this?

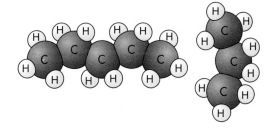

Another word for burning

We use the word 'burn' to mean different things.

10 Copy and complete the sentence.

The kind of burning when something joins with oxygen and releases energy is called _____.

Acids burn your skin.

Fuels release energy when they burn. This kind of burning in oxygen is called **combustion**.

What you need to remember [Copy and complete using the **key words**]

Burning fuels – where do they go?

When fuels burn they react with _____ from the air.

The new substances that are produced are mainly _____ that escape into the air.

The atoms in fuels join up with oxygen atoms to form compounds called _____.

When hydrocarbons burn:

- hydrogen atoms join up with oxygen atoms to make _____ molecules

- carbon atoms join up with oxygen atoms to make _____ _____ molecules.

Another word for burning is _____.

20

Dangers with fuels

Fuels such as methane, petrol and diesel are hydrocarbons.

When they burn in plenty of oxygen they produce water and carbon dioxide.

1 Atoms from a burning hydrocarbon join up with other atoms to make water and carbon dioxide.

   (a) What other atoms do they join up with?

   (b) Where do these other atoms come from?

If there is not enough oxygen, the hydrocarbons don't burn properly. They then produce smoke and a poisonous gas.

> ## REMEMBER
>
> Hydrocarbon molecules contain hydrogen atoms and carbon atoms.
>
> When hydrocarbons burn in air:
>
> - hydrogen atoms join up with oxygen atoms to produce water
> - carbon atoms join up with oxygen atoms to produce carbon dioxide.

▨ What makes a Bunsen flame smoky?

The diagrams show two Bunsen burners.

One is burning with a clean flame. The other is burning with a smoky flame.

2 Copy and complete the table.

air hole _____	plenty of oxygen	clear, _____ flame
air hole _____	shortage of oxygen	smoky, _____ flame

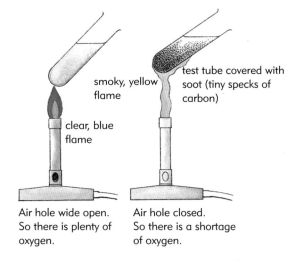

smoky, yellow flame

test tube covered with soot (tiny specks of carbon)

clear, blue flame

Air hole wide open. So there is plenty of oxygen.

Air hole closed. So there is a shortage of oxygen.

3 What is there in the yellow flame to make it smoky?

▨ Problems with diesel engines

The diagram shows what can happen when a lorry with a faulty diesel engine is going up a steep hill.

4 (a) What happens to the exhaust of the faulty engine?

   (b) Why do you think this happens?

   (c) Write down two problems that this can cause.

the exhaust is very smoky

the driver has to make a lot of diesel fuel go to the engine

The small specks of carbon from diesel exhausts:
- make the air very dirty
- can make it difficult for people with asthma to breathe

Earth materials

What poisonous gas can be produced when things burn?

When there is plenty of oxygen, the carbon in a fuel burns to produce **carbon dioxide**.

When there is less oxygen, a poisonous gas called **carbon monoxide** is also produced.

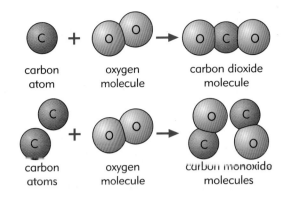

5 Look at the diagrams.

Then describe the difference between a molecule of carbon monoxide and a molecule of carbon dioxide.

6 Explain why carbon monoxide is poisonous.

Burning fuels safely at home

Many people heat their homes with gas fires.

Every year, dozens of people die in their homes because of carbon monoxide poisoning.

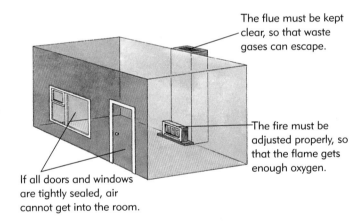

The flue must be kept clear, so that waste gases can escape.

The fire must be adjusted properly, so that the flame gets enough oxygen.

If all doors and windows are tightly sealed, air cannot get into the room.

7 Write down three reasons why this can happen.

Carbon monoxide

It is colourless – you can't see it.

It is odourless – you can't smell it.

But it is very poisonous.

It can kill you.

It gets into your red blood cells and stops them carrying oxygen to the cells in your body.

About $\frac{1}{5}$ of air is oxygen.

What you need to remember [Copy and complete using the **key words**]

Dangers with fuels

When hydrocarbons burn completely, the carbon atoms join up with oxygen atoms to make _____ _____.

If there isn't enough oxygen you can get:

- lots of tiny bits of _____.
- a poisonous gas called _____ _____.

21

It's raining acid

Acids are dangerous substances. We know that they can 'eat away' at some things.

1 (a) What has happened to the statue in the photograph?

(b) What has caused this to happen to the statue?

Acid rain is a serious problem in many countries including Britain. As well as damaging buildings, acid rain can harm animals and plants.

2 Write down <u>two</u> ways acid rain can harm living things.

We need to prevent acid rain from forming. To do this we have to understand what causes it.

Acid rain can kill trees and the fish in lakes.

What turns our rain into acid?

When fuels burn they react with oxygen. Atoms in the fuel join with oxygen atoms in the air. New substances called oxides are made.

Most fuels contain carbon atoms.

3 What new substance do the carbon atoms make when a fuel burns?

Many fuels also contain some sulphur atoms.

4 (a) What new substance do the sulphur atoms make when the fuel burns?

(b) Write down a word equation for this reaction.

Sulphur dioxide is a gas that can turn rain into acid.

carbon atom	oxygen molecule		carbon dioxide molecule

sulphur atom	oxygen molecule		sulphur dioxide molecule

We can also write these reactions like this:

$$C(s) + O_2(g) \longrightarrow CO_2(g)$$

$$S(s) + O_2(g) \longrightarrow SO_2(g)$$

(s) = solid, (g) = gas

Earth materials

How sulphur dioxide makes acid rain

5 Copy and complete the following sentences.

Some fuels contain sulphur.

When we burn these fuels we make a _____ called sulphur dioxide.

This goes into the _____.

The sulphur dioxide reacts with oxygen and then dissolves in droplets of _____.

This makes an acid called _____ _____.

Eventually the acidic droplets in the clouds fall as _____ _____.

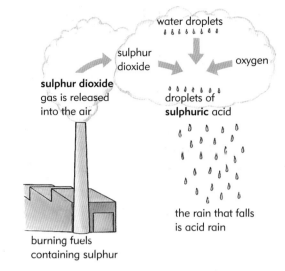

How rain turns into acid.

Acid rain does not usually fall where it is made. Winds can blow the 'acid clouds' for hundreds of kilometres before they fall as rain.

Don't just blame sulphur

It's not just the sulphur in fuels that causes acid rain. When we burn things at high temperatures the **nitrogen** in the air can join up with oxygen. This happens inside car engines.

6 What new substances are made when the nitrogen atoms join up with oxygen atoms?

7 What substance is produced when nitrogen oxides dissolve in droplets of water?

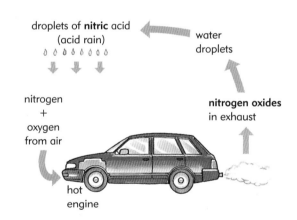

What you need to remember [Copy and complete using the **key words**]

It's raining acid

Acid rain can harm buildings and living things.
When we burn fuels that contain sulphur we make the gas called _____

_____.

This gas dissolves in water droplets to make _____ acid.
The heat from burning fuels makes oxygen and _____ from the air react together. This makes gases called _____ _____.
These gases dissolve in water to produce _____ acid.

22

How are we changing the air around us?

If you could travel back in time 200 million years, the Earth would look very different. But the air would be almost the **same**. The amount of each gas in the air has hardly changed for millions of years.

The pie chart shows you how much of each gas there is in the air.

1 Copy and complete the following sentences.

The two main gases in the air are _____, about _____, and _____, about _____.

There is also a small amount of the _____ gases and an even smaller amount of _____ _____.

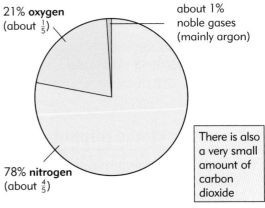

21% **oxygen**
(about $\frac{1}{5}$)

about 1% noble gases (mainly argon)

78% **nitrogen**
(about $\frac{4}{5}$)

There is also a very small amount of carbon dioxide

What's in the air?

■ How does burning fuels affect the air?

When we burn fuels like coal, gas and oil we put **carbon dioxide** into the air. The graph shows how this is affecting the amount of carbon dioxide in the air.

2 How much carbon dioxide was there in the air until about 1800?

3 What has happened to the carbon dioxide in the air since then? (Use figures in your answer.)

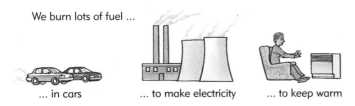

We burn lots of fuel ...

... in cars   ... to make electricity   ... to keep warm

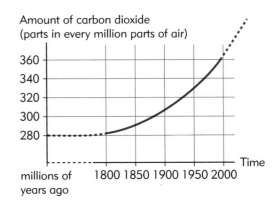

Amount of carbon dioxide
(parts in every million parts of air)

360
340
320
300
280

millions of years ago

1800 1850 1900 1950 2000

Time

4 Why do you think the amount of carbon dioxide in the air has changed in this way?

■ What effect does the extra carbon dioxide have?

There is still only a very small amount of carbon dioxide in the air. But it has a big effect on the temperature of the Earth.

Earth materials

5 (a) Read the newspaper article then copy and complete the following sentences.

We put _____ _____ gas into the air when we burn fuels.

This is causing the _____ of the Earth's air to rise.

We call this effect _____ _____.

(b) If the Earth's air gets hotter it will cause many things to change.
Write down <u>two</u> of these changes.

Why does carbon dioxide make the Earth warmer?

Carbon dioxide helps to keep the Earth warm. It works in a similar way to a greenhouse. The diagrams show how.

6 Copy and complete the following sentences.

Energy from the _____ can pass through the air to the Earth.

But _____ _____ makes it hard for the energy to get out again.

The carbon dioxide works just like the _____ in a greenhouse.

We say that carbon dioxide is a **greenhouse** gas. Carbon dioxide makes the Earth a warmer place. But too much carbon dioxide can make it too warm.

'It's a heat wave'

Weather experts say that the hot summer is likely to continue for a few more weeks. Scientists think that the record temperatures might be the effect of **global warming**.

Dr Simon Gray said today '... there is no doubt in my mind that our summers are getting hotter. It could be due to the large amounts of carbon dioxide gas we're producing.'

Warmer temperatures could cause serious problems.

'I think we will see more flooding in some countries while others will become too dry for people to live', he said yesterday.

Farmers might need to grow different crops. The sea level could rise and flood many cities around the world.

Energy from the Sun can easily pass through the air.

But carbon dioxide makes it harder for the energy to get out again.

So the surface of the Earth is warmer.

Energy from the Sun can pass through glass.

But energy from inside a greenhouse cannot easily get out again. So the greenhouse gets warmer.

What you need to remember [Copy and complete using the **key words**]

How are we changing the air around us?

The air around us has been almost the _____ for millions of years.

Nearly $\frac{4}{5}$ of the air is _____ and just over $\frac{1}{5}$ is _____.

When we burn fuels we make large amounts of _____ _____ gas.

Too much carbon dioxide in the air could make the temperature of the Earth rise.

We call this _____ _____.

We say that carbon dioxide is a _____ gas.

1

Two kinds of stuff

We all need to sort things out from time to time. In your bedroom you might have a 'sorting system'.

Scientists like to sort things out because it makes those things easier to study. One way scientists sort things is into **solids** and **liquids**.

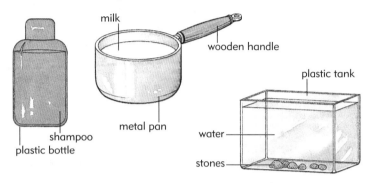

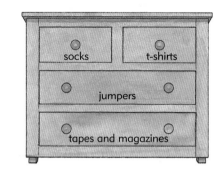

1 Write down lists of the different solids and the different liquids you can find in the picture above.

What's the difference between solids and liquids?

It's easy to <u>sort</u> things into solids and liquids. It's not so easy to say <u>how</u> you decide which group they belong to.

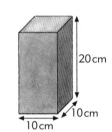

2 Look at the diagrams.

(a) What <u>two</u> things will a liquid do that a solid won't do?

(b) The jug and glasses are solid. They stay the same shape. What happens to the shape of the orange juice in the jug and glasses?

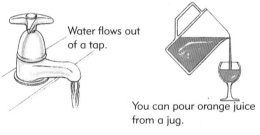

You can pour orange juice from a jug.

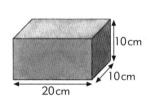

The volume of this brick is always 2000 cm^3.

How much room?

A solid always stays the same **shape**. It always takes up the same amount of space. We say that it stays the same **volume**.

The diagram shows what happens when you pour a 500 ml bottle of 'Coke' into different containers.

3 Copy and complete the following sentence.

The 'Coke' looks different in each of the containers but its _____ stays exactly the same.

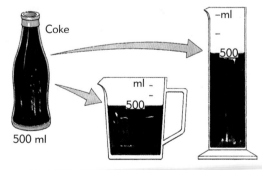

A millilitre (ml) is the same as a centimetre (cm) cubed.
1 ml = 1 cm^3

All change

If you make water cold enough it turns into ice. We say the water **freezes**. If you make ice warm enough it turns back into water. We say the ice **melts**. Many other solids can also change into liquids and change back again.

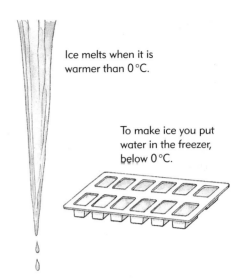

Ice melts when it is warmer than 0 °C.

To make ice you put water in the freezer, below 0 °C.

4 Look at the diagrams then copy and complete these sentences.

When a substance melts it turns from a _____ into a _____. When a substance freezes it changes from a _____ to a _____.

The temperature at which a solid melts is called the **melting point** of that solid.

5 What is the melting point of

(a) ice?

(b) gold?

To make candles, you melt wax, pour it into a mould and then let it cool down. The wax melts at 80 °C when you heat it up.

6 At what temperature will the wax freeze when you cool it down?

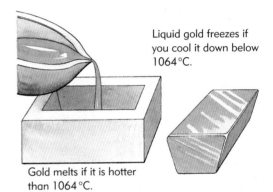

Liquid gold freezes if you cool it down below 1064 °C.

Gold melts if it is hotter than 1064 °C.

What you need to remember [Copy and complete using the **key words**]

Two kinds of stuff

One of the ways scientists sort materials is into _____ and

_____.

Solids stay the same _____ and always have the same volume.
We can pour liquids into different containers. The liquid takes the shape of the container but it still has the same _____.
When a solid turns into a liquid, we say that it _____.
The temperature at which it does this is called its _____ _____.
When a liquid turns into a solid, we say that it _____.

2

Stuff you hardly know is there

You can't see the air around you but there really is something there. You notice it only when you see what it can do.

1 Look at the picture.

Write down <u>three</u> things which tell you that air is not just empty space.

Air isn't a solid or a liquid. Air is a **gas**.

Different sorts of gases

There are many different gases. The diagrams show some of the gases and what they are used for.

Helium is a very light gas.

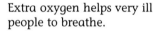

Extra oxygen helps very ill people to breathe.

We burn methane gas in our homes.

Fizzy drinks contain carbon dioxide gas.

2 Copy out this table.

Name of gas	What it is used for
helium	filling balloons

Use the pictures to help you fill in the table. The first row has been filled in for you.

What's special about gases?

A gas **spreads** out to fill all the space that it can. Gases are also special because you can squash them into a smaller amount of space. You can **compress** a gas.

Look at the pictures.

3 Describe an example of a gas spreading out all over the place.

4 Describe an example where a lot of gas is pushed into a much smaller space.

The gas from a stink bomb soon spreads all over the room.

Each time you push the pump you squeeze more air into the ball.

Structure and bonding

■ How heavy are gases?

We can weigh solids, liquids and gases.

5 Look in the table.

 (a) Which are the two lightest substances?

 (b) Which group do they belong to, solid, liquid or gas?

 (c) Which gas is heavier, carbon dioxide or air?

Substance	Solid, liquid or gas	Mass in g of 1000 cm³
stone	solid	2400
steel	solid	8000
water	liquid	1000
mercury	liquid	13 600
air	gas	about 1
carbon dioxide	gas	about 2

■ Where do they go?

Sometimes liquids seem to disappear. If you heat up a liquid it will change into a gas or vapour. We call this **evaporating**. If you cool a gas or vapour then it will change back into a liquid. We call this **condensing**.

6 Copy and complete the following sentences.

When water evaporates it changes from a _____ to a _____. An example of this is _____.

Windows 'steam up' when water _____ condenses on them.

■ Solids, liquids and gases – that's all there is

Everything is a solid, a liquid, a gas or a mixture of these. These three sorts of stuff are called the three **states** of matter.

What you need to remember [Copy and complete using the **key words**]

Stuff you hardly know is there

You can squeeze a _____ into a smaller space; you can _____ it.

A gas _____ out to fill all the space it can.

When a liquid changes to a gas we call it _____.

When a gas turns into a liquid we call it _____.

Solids, liquids and gases are the three _____ of matter.

Structure and bonding

Making up a model

3

Making models helps us to explain things. Scientists use a model to explain the differences between solids, liquids and gases. They imagine that everything is made up from tiny **particles** much too small to see.

REMEMBER

Solids always stay the same **shape** and take up the same amount of space. You can put a liquid into a differently shaped container, but it still takes up the same amount of space.

▥ Particles in a solid

The particles in a solid are very **close** together, a bit like apples in a box. Each particle touches the particles next to it.

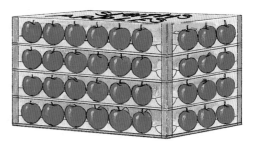

1 Why can't you squeeeze a solid into a smaller space?

Some solids form regular shapes called crystals. This is because the particles are arranged in very neat rows. A cutter can slice through the rows of particles.

2 Look at the diagram.

   (a) Draw the two pieces that the crystal splits into.

   (b) Why is it so easy to split the crystal with a blade?

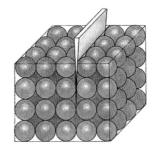

To cut a crystal we use a sharp blade. The blade splits the crystal between two layers of particles.

Jewellers cut diamonds with a steel blade to make them sparkle more in the light.

They can do this even though diamonds are harder than steel.

3 Explain why a steel blade can cut diamond.

A steel blade can be used to cut diamonds so that they sparkle.

▥ Particles that stay in their places

A solid always stays the same shape. This is because the particles <u>stay in their places</u>, they do not move around. The particles do not stay perfectly still but they **vibrate**.

4 Look at the diagram. What does the word 'vibrate' mean?

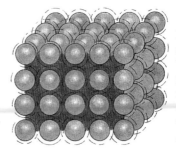

Particles in a solid. The particles move a little from side to side (vibrate) but they do not change places.

Structure and bonding

Particles in liquids

Liquids always take up the same space. This is because the particles in a liquid are very **close** together, like they are in solids. We cannot squeeze them together any closer.

The diagram shows how the particles in a liquid are <u>different</u> from those in a solid.

5 Copy and complete this sentence.

We can pour liquids because _____.

Particles that seem to disappear

If we put sugar in a mug of tea the grains seem to disappear. We know that the sugar is still there because we can taste it. We say that the sugar **dissolves**.

The diagram shows how we can explain this.

6 Copy and complete the following sentence.

When sugar dissolves the _____ of sugar spread out through the _____ of water.

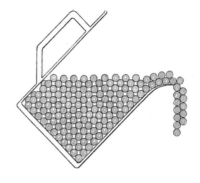

Particles in a liquid.
The particles can **move** over each other. This is why liquids take the shape of the container.

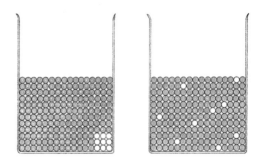

The sugar particles break away from each other. They mix in with the water **particles**.

What you need to remember [Copy and complete using the **key words**]

Making up a model

Scientists believe that everything is made up of tiny _____.

Solids and liquids take up the same amount of space because their particles are _____ together.

Particles in solids can only _____ (move about from side to side), so the solid stays the same _____.

You can pour a liquid because the particles _____ over each other.

Some solids seem to disappear if we put them in a liquid.

We say that the solid _____ in the liquid. The solid particles separate and spread out through the _____ of the liquid.

4

A particle model of gases

Everything is made up from small particles, too tiny to see. Particles in solids and liquids are close together. But what about gases?

Gases are very **light** compared to solids and liquids. This is because gases are made up from particles that are a long way apart. Gases are also called vapours.

1 A tub of solid ice cream is much heavier than the same tub full of air.

   Use the idea of particles to explain why.

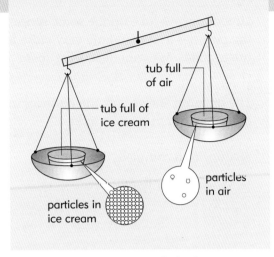

The particles in air are much further apart than the particles in ice cream.

Gases have weight

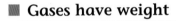

Although gases are very light we can still weigh them.

2 Look at the diagrams. Then copy and complete the table.

mass of flask full of air	_____ g
mass of empty flask	_____ g
mass of 500 cm³ of air	_____ g

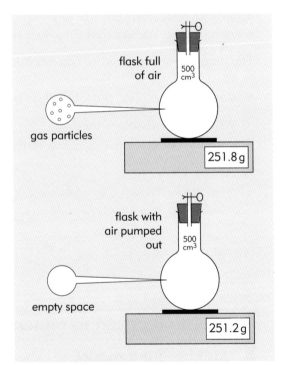

3 Use the bar chart to find

   (a) <u>two</u> gases that are lighter than air.

   (b) <u>two</u> gases that are heavier than air.

   (c) the mass of one litre (1000 cm³) of air.

A litre of water has a mass of 1000 g.

4 Copy and complete the following sentence.

   A litre of air is much lighter than a litre of water because the particles are much _____ _____.

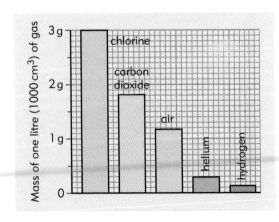

Structure and bonding

Squeezing gases

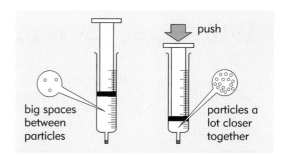

Squeezing a gas into less space.

We can squeeze gases into a smaller space. Now we know about the particles we can explain why gases are so 'squashy'.

5 Copy and complete the following sentences.

There are big _____ between the particles in a gas like air. So it is quite easy to press them _____ together.

If we squash, or **compress**, gases very hard we can squeeze them into smaller containers. This makes them easier to carry around with us.

6 Look at the photographs. Then copy and complete the table.

Compressed gas	What it is used for

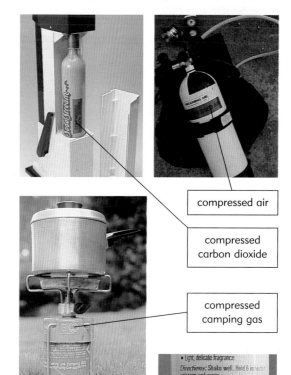

compressed air

compressed carbon dioxide

compressed camping gas

this means highly flammable

Taking care with aerosol cans

Aerosol cans often contain gases. When the can seems empty there is usually some gas left inside. The can must not be thrown on to a fire or the gas inside will heat up. The gas will spread out more as it gets hotter. This might make the can explode.

7 Look at the picture of an aerosol can.

Write down <u>two</u> reasons why you shouldn't throw 'empty' cans on to a fire.

What you need to remember [Copy and complete using the **key words**]

A particle model of gases

We can weigh gases but they are very _____ compared to solids or liquids.
This is because the particles in a gas are a long way apart.
We can squash or _____ gases more than solids or liquids.
This is also because the gas particles are so spread out.

5

Why gases get everywhere

Gases spread out to fill all the **space** they can. Sometimes this is pleasant. But it can also do a lot of harm.

'Mmm, that smells GOOD!'

Poisonous gases were used in the First World War.

1 Write down

   (a) <u>two</u> examples of gases that do harm when they spread.

   (b) <u>one</u> pleasant example of gases spreading out.

We can explain why gases spread out using the particle model.

Gas particles move very fast

The particles of a gas are not just a long way apart. They also **move** about very quickly.

The diagram shows gas particles inside a container.

2 What happens to the gas particles when they reach the side of the container?

3 What do you think would happen if the container wasn't there?

Gases spread out because their particles can move about so easily. We call this **diffusion**.

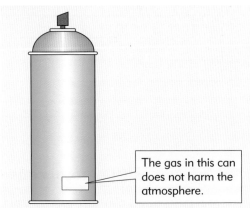

The gas in this can does not harm the atmosphere.

Aerosol cans often have a label like this. This is because in the past, many aerosol cans used CFC gases. These gases <u>did</u> harm the atmosphere.

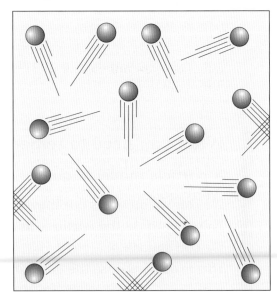

Structure and bonding

▥ Watching gases diffuse

Many gases have no smell. Most are also invisible so it is hard to tell if diffusion is happening. We can see bromine vapour because it is brown.

The photographs show how bromine diffuses into the air.

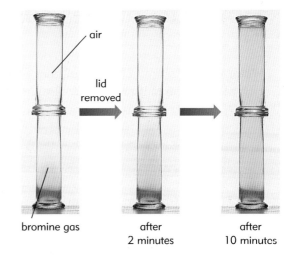

bromine gas   after   after
                     2 minutes   10 minutes

4 Copy and complete the following sentences.

The bromine gradually _____ into the air.
After _____ minutes the bromine and the air are completely mixed.

The diagrams show the particles of bromine and air.

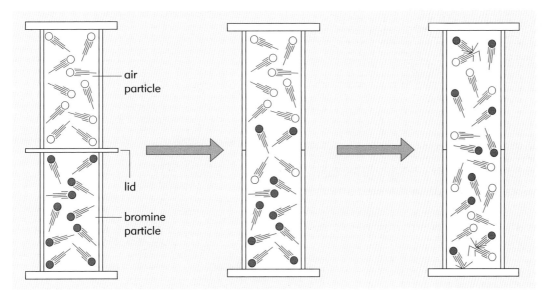

5 Explain why the bromine particles and the air particles become mixed.

6 The bromine and air particles move very fast. But it still takes a few minutes for them to mix completely. Why is this?

What you need to remember [Copy and complete using the **key words**]

Why gases get everywhere

Gases spread out to fill all the _____ they can.
This is because gas particles _____ about very fast.
We call the spreading out of gases _____.

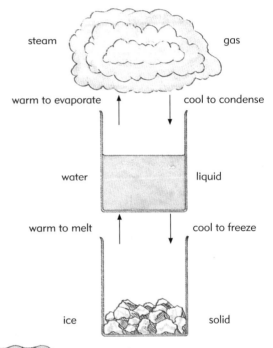

6

How substances can change their state

Water is often a liquid. But it can also be a solid or a gas. Many other substances can also be a solid, liquid or gas. What state they are in depends on the temperature.

1 What do we call water

(a) when it is in the solid state?

(b) when it is in the gas state?

2 Copy and complete the table.

Change of state	What we call the change
solid into liquid	the solid has _____
liquid into solid	the liquid has _____
liquid into gas	the liquid has _____
gas into liquid	the gas has _____

> **REMEMBER**
>
> Substances can be solids, liquids or gases. We call these the three states of matter.

▓ Why do solids melt?

If we heat up a solid we are giving the particles more **energy**. They can move from side to side more quickly. When they get enough energy some of the particles can move away from the others. They are now free to move because they have more energy.

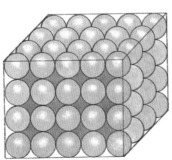

Solid. Particles in fixed positions.

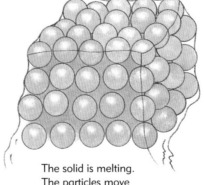

The solid is melting. The particles move over each other.

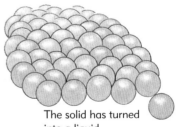

The solid has turned into a liquid.

3 Look at the diagram then copy and complete the following sentences.

If we make a solid hot enough then all of the _____ separate from each other. The solid turns into a _____.

The particles are then free to _____ about all around each other.

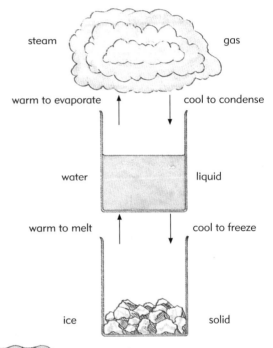

steam   gas

warm to evaporate   cool to condense

water   liquid

warm to melt   cool to freeze

ice   solid

Structure and bonding

Why do liquids evaporate?

Liquids can evaporate even when they are quite cool. If you spill petrol on to a garage floor it 'dries up' quickly. The petrol **evaporates**.

We can make liquids evaporate more **quickly** if we heat them up.

4 Look at the diagram.

   (a) What happens to the particles in a liquid if we heat them up?

   (b) What happens to the particles in a liquid when they gain enough energy?

   (c) What do the escaped particles form?

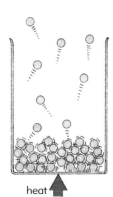

If we heat up a liquid the particles move more quickly.

If the particles have enough energy they escape. The particles now form a gas.

What happens when a liquid boils?

If we heat a liquid its temperature will rise. If we keep on heating it, the liquid will **boil**. When it is boiling the temperature of the liquid stays the same.

5 The diagram shows what happens when a liquid boils.

   (a) How can you <u>see</u> when a liquid is boiling?

   (b) Where have the bubbles of gas come from?

6 A kettle is switched on to make a pot of tea. The graph shows the temperature inside the kettle. Copy and complete the following sentences.

   The kettle boiled at _____ °C. It took _____ seconds for the water to boil.

7 What does the energy supplied to the kettle do:

   (a) during the first 50 seconds?

   (b) after 50 seconds?

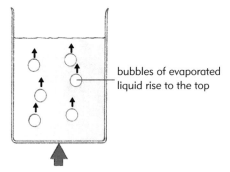

bubbles of evaporated liquid rise to the top

A boiling liquid.

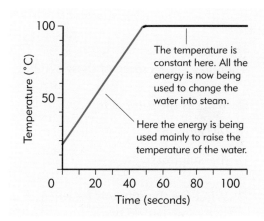

The temperature is constant here. All the energy is now being used to change the water into steam.

Here the energy is being used mainly to raise the temperature of the water.

What you need to remember [Copy and complete using the **key words**]

How substances can change their state

If we heat up a solid the particles gain more _____. The particles then start to break away from each other; the solid is now _____.

The particles in a liquid can escape if they get enough energy. When this happens we say the liquid _____.

If we heat up a liquid the particles can escape more _____.

Large bubbles of gas form in a liquid when we make the liquid _____.

7

Elements and compounds

All chemical substances are made from tiny **atoms**. There are just over 90 different kinds of atoms in nature. If a substance is made from just one kind of atom, we call it an **element**.

Carbon is an element. It contains only carbon atoms.

1 How many elements do you think there are? Give a reason for your answer.

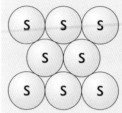

Sulphur is an element. It contains only sulphur atoms.

Using letters to stand for elements

We can save time and space by using our initials instead of writing our full name. A post code makes it easier to deliver letters to the right address. In science we can do the same with the names of the elements. We call these letters **symbols**.

Kenneth Gill's briefcase.

The table shows some of these symbols.

2 What is the symbol for

(a) carbon?

(b) sulphur?

3 What are the symbols for calcium and for silicon?

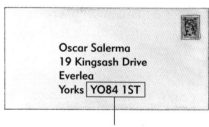

This is the post code.

Some of the symbols we use come from the old names of the elements.

4 Copy and complete the following table.

Element	Old name	Symbol
	cuprum	
sodium		

Element	Symbol we use	
carbon	C	
calcium	Ca	
copper	Cu	from cuprum, the old name
nitrogen	N	
neon	Ne	
sulphur	S	
silicon	Si	
sodium	Na	from natrium, the old name

What are compounds?

When atoms of different elements join together we get substances called **compounds**. Most substances are compounds.

The diagrams show some compounds. Each compound has its own **formula**. The formula of a compound tells us two things:

- it tells us which elements are in the compound

- it tells us how many atoms of each element there are in the compound.

5 Copy the table. Then complete it to include all of the compounds shown on this page.

Name of compound	Formula	Atoms in the compound
carbon dioxide	CO_2	1 carbon atom, 2 oxygen atoms
water		
ammonia		
calcium oxide		
copper sulphate		
calcium hydroxide		

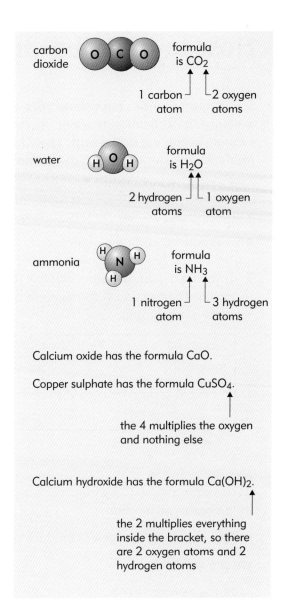

carbon dioxide — formula is CO_2

1 carbon atom — 2 oxygen atoms

water — formula is H_2O

2 hydrogen atoms — 1 oxygen atom

ammonia — formula is NH_3

1 nitrogen atom — 3 hydrogen atoms

Calcium oxide has the formula CaO.

Copper sulphate has the formula $CuSO_4$.

the 4 multiplies the oxygen and nothing else

Calcium hydroxide has the formula $Ca(OH)_2$.

the 2 multiplies everything inside the bracket, so there are 2 oxygen atoms and 2 hydrogen atoms

---

What you need to remember [Copy and complete using the **key words**]

Elements and compounds

All substances are made from tiny _____.

If the substance has atoms that are all of one type, we call it an _____.

Substances made from atoms of different elements joined together are called

_____.

We use letters to stand for elements. We call these _____.

The _____ of a compound tells us which atoms are in the compound.

[If you are given the formula of a compound, you should be able to say how many atoms there are of each element in the compound.]

8

How to describe chemical reactions

The diagrams on this page show three different chemical reactions. In a chemical reaction the **reactants** are the substances you use at the start. These turn into **products**, the substances left at the end.

In the barbecue reaction:

- the reactants are oxygen and carbon

- the product is carbon dioxide

1 Copy the headings. Then complete the table to include the reaction with magnesium ribbon shown in the photographs.

Reactant(s)	Product(s)
carbon oxygen	carbon dioxide

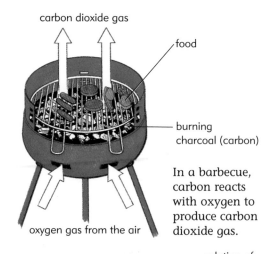

carbon dioxide gas
food
burning charcoal (carbon)
oxygen gas from the air

In a barbecue, carbon reacts with oxygen to produce carbon dioxide gas.

Writing word equations

In the barbecue reaction:

carbon reacts with oxygen to produce carbon dioxide

We can write this:

carbon + oxygen ⟶ carbon dioxide

We call this a **word equation**.

2 Write down a word equation for the reaction between zinc and copper sulphate shown in the photographs.

Understanding symbol equations

There is another way to write down what happens in a chemical reaction. We can replace the <u>name</u> of each reactant and product with a **formula**.

For the barbecue reaction the two kinds of equation look like this:

carbon + oxygen ⟶ carbon dioxide

C + O_2 ⟶ CO_2

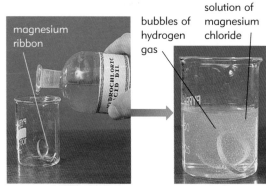

magnesium ribbon
bubbles of hydrogen gas
solution of magnesium chloride

Magnesium reacts with dilute hydrochloric acid to produce hydrogen gas and a solution of magnesium chloride.

copper sulphate solution
zinc powder
zinc sulphate solution
copper metal powder

Zinc reacts with copper sulphate solution to produce zinc sulphate solution and copper metal.

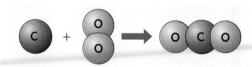

Carbon reacts with oxygen to produce carbon dioxide.

Structure and bonding

We call the second one a **symbol equation**.

The box shows the symbol equations for the other two reactions shown on the last page.

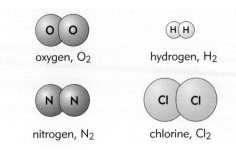

$$Mg + 2HCl \longrightarrow MgCl_2 + H_2$$
$$Zn + CuSO_4 \longrightarrow ZnSO_4 + Cu$$

3 Copy each of the symbol equations from the box. Write the name of each reactant and product underneath the right formula.

The atoms of elements that are gases often go round in pairs.

4 Write down the names of <u>three</u> gases, besides oxygen, with atoms that go round in pairs.

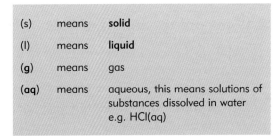

oxygen, O_2 hydrogen, H_2

nitrogen, N_2 chlorine, Cl_2

Oxygen is a gas. Oxygen atoms go round in pairs. The atoms of some other gases also go round in pairs.

Adding state symbols

Reactants and products can be solids, liquids or gases, or can be dissolved in water. We can show this by using state symbols.

In the barbecue reaction:

carbon is a solid

oxygen and carbon dioxide are both gases

We can now write the equation like this:

$$C(s) + O_2(g) \longrightarrow CO_2(g)$$

5 Add state symbols to the symbol equations for the other two reactions. Remember that solutions need the state symbol (aq).

(s)	means	**solid**
(l)	means	**liquid**
(g)	means	gas
(aq)	means	aqueous, this means solutions of substances dissolved in water e.g. HCl(aq)

What state symbols mean.

What you need to remember [Copy and complete using the **key words**]

How to describe chemical reactions

We can describe a chemical reaction using a **word** _____.
The substances that react are the _____.
The new substances that are produced are the _____.
We can replace the names of each reactant and product by writing its _____.
The equation for the reaction is now called a _____ **equation**.
In a symbol equation, (s) stands for _____, (l) stands for _____,
_____ stands for gas, _____ stands for aqueous solution.

[You should now be able to:
■ write word equations for reactions you know about
■ explain what a symbol equation means in words.]

9 The alkali metals – a chemical family

The picture shows what happens when a small piece of potassium metal is put in some water. Lithium and sodium react in the same sort of way in this and other reactions. So we say that these elements are all part of the same chemical family. We call this family the **alkali metals**.

The diagram shows part of a table of elements. We call this table the Periodic Table.

1 The alkali metals are all in the same Group of the Periodic Table. Which Group is it?

What are the alkali metals like?

Alkali metals are like other metals in many ways. There are also some differences.

2 Write down <u>three</u> ways in which alkali metals are the same as other metals.

3 Write down <u>two</u> ways in which alkali metals are different from other metals.

Alkali metals are very **reactive**. This is why we store them under oil, away from the air and water.

4 Copy and complete the following sentences.

Alkali metals are stored under _____.

This stops them reacting with _____ or _____.

Why do we call them alkali metals?

Alkali metals all react very fast with cold water. They fizz and move around on the water as they react. A gas called **hydrogen** is produced.

This is the word equation for the reaction of sodium with water:

sodium + water ⟶ hydrogen + sodium hydroxide

The sodium **hydroxide** dissolves in the water as the sodium reacts. Sodium hydroxide solution is **alkaline**.

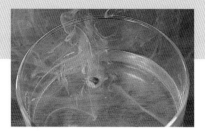

The potassium darts about as it reacts with the water, making it fizz.

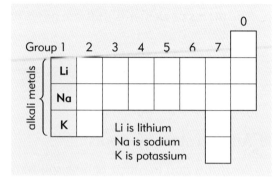

Group 1	2	3	4	5	6	7	0
Li							
Na							
K							

alkali metals

Li is lithium
Na is sodium
K is potassium

Most metals are hard, but your teacher can cut alkali metals with a knife, as easily as cutting cheese.

Alkali metals are shiny when you first cut them, just like other metals.

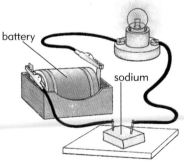

battery
sodium

Like other metals, alkali metals conduct electricity and heat, but they melt more easily than most other metals.

Structure and bonding

The diagram shows what happens when sodium reacts with water.

5 How do we know that sodium hydroxide solution is alkaline?

6 Why does the water fizz as it reacts with the sodium?

7 Potassium reacts with cold water in the same sort of way as sodium. Write a word equation for this reaction.

8 Potassium gives an alkali with water. What is the name of this alkali?

The sodium moves about on top of the water, making it fizz.

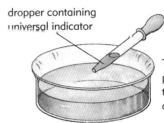

dropper containing universal indicator

The indicator turns purple, which shows that the solution is alkaline.

All alkali metal hydroxides dissolve in water to give alkaline solutions. This is why we call these metals the alkali metals.

Do alkali metals react with other elements?

Not all of the elements are metals. Oxygen is an example of a non-metal. Some **non-metals** will react with metals to make compounds.

Hot sodium metal reacts violently with oxygen gas. This is the word equation for the reaction.

sodium + oxygen ⟶ **sodium oxide**

The other alkali metals react with oxygen in the same way.

9 Write down the word equation for the reaction between lithium and oxygen.

Alkali metals also react with a family of non-metal elements called the halogens.

oxygen gas

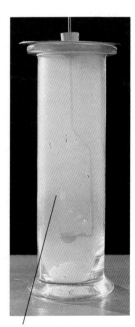

hot sodium metal

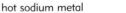

sodium oxide fumes fill the jar

What you need to remember [Copy and complete using the **key words**]

The alkali metals – a chemical family

The elements in Group 1 are called the _____ _____.

We need to keep them under oil because they are very _____.

Alkali metals react with water to produce _____ gas.

A solution of the alkali metal _____ is also produced.

An indicator shows that the solution is _____.

Alkali metals react with some _____, such as oxygen. For example:

sodium + oxygen ⟶ _____ _____

Structure and bonding

10

The halogens – another chemical family

We have already learnt about one family of elements, the alkali metals. The alkali metals are all in Group 1 of the Periodic Table of the elements.

In **Group 7** there is another family of elements. We call this family of elements the **halogens**.

1 Write down the names of <u>four</u> elements in the halogen family.

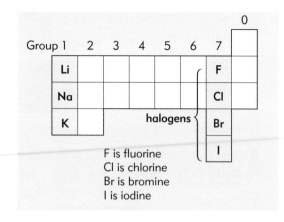

F is fluorine
Cl is chlorine
Br is bromine
I is iodine

■ What are the halogens like?

The halogens are non-metals. The diagrams show what some of the halogens look like at room temperature.

2 At room temperature:

(a) which halogen is a solid?

(b) which <u>two</u> halogens are gases?

(c) which halogen is a liquid that gives off a gas?

The halogens are all coloured when they are gases. Other elements that are gases have no colour, so we say they are colourless. An example is oxygen gas.

3 Copy and complete the table. The first row has been filled in for you.

Name of the halogen	Colour of gas
fluorine	pale yellow

Fluorine.

Chlorine.

Bromine.

Bromine.

heat

Iodine crystals produce iodine gas when you heat them.

Iodine crystals.

fluorine   chlorine   bromine   iodine

4 Look at the diagram. Copy and complete the following sentence.

Halogen _____ contain pairs of halogen atoms.

Halogen atoms are joined together in pairs. We call these pairs **molecules**.

Structure and bonding

Halogens can react with metals

Halogens react with metals to form compounds called **halides**. Halides are part of a family of compounds called **salts**. The word 'halogen' means 'salt maker'. The diagram shows how you can make ordinary salt, the kind you can put on your food.

5 What is the chemical name for ordinary salt?

6 Which two elements are in ordinary salt?

7 Write down a word equation for the reaction to make salt.

The other alkali metals react with halogens in the same kind of way. The box shows how we name the salts.

8 What do we call the salt made from:

(a) potassium and iodine?

(b) lithium and bromine?

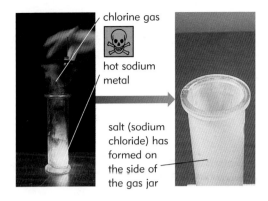

chlorine gas

hot sodium metal

salt (sodium chloride) has formed on the side of the gas jar

$$2Na(s) + Cl_2(g) \longrightarrow 2NaCl(s)$$

The names we give to salts from the halogens

fluorine gives salts called fluorides

chlorine gives salts called chlorides

bromine gives salts called bromides

iodine gives salts called iodides

Halogens can react with other non-metals

Halogen atoms can join up with atoms of other **non-metals** such as hydrogen and carbon. The diagrams show some of the new compounds that can be made.

9 Write down the name and the formula of a halogen compound that we use to make a plastic.

10 (a) Draw a molecule that contains <u>two</u> different halogens.

(b) For what was this material once used?

hydrogen chloride — This gas dissolves in water to make an acid.

vinyl chloride — We use this to make a plastic called PVC.

a CFC compound — This was used in fridges and in aerosol cans as well. 'CFC' stands for 'chlorofluorocarbon'.

Some compounds of the halogens with other non-metals.

What you need to remember [Copy and complete using the **key words**]

The halogens – another chemical family

The elements that are 'salt makers' are called _____.

These elements are all in **Group** _____ of the Periodic Table.

Atoms of the halogens join up in pairs. We call these pairs _____.

Halogens react with metals to form compounds we call _____. These compounds are part of a family of compounds called _____.

Halogens also react with other _____-_____ such as hydrogen and carbon.

11

What are atoms made of?

Looking inside atoms

The diagram shows what is inside a helium atom. In the centre of the atom is the **nucleus**.
Electrons move in the space around the nucleus.

1 (a) What <u>two</u> sorts of particles do you find in the nucleus of an atom?

(b) What is the same about these two particles?

(c) What is different?

2 Copy and complete the table.

Name of particle	Mass	Electrical charge
proton	1	+1
neutron		
electron		

3 The complete helium atom has no electrical charge overall. Why is this?

The number of protons is always the same as the number of electrons in an atom. This means that the positive and negative charges balance in an atom.

The symbols that show what atoms contain

This diagram tells you everything you need to know about a helium atom.

4 Copy and complete the following sentences.

The helium atom has _____ protons.

So it must also have _____ electrons.

The helium atom has a mass number of _____.

So it must contain two _____ in its nucleus.

The proton number of an atom tells us what element the atom is. So an atom with 2 protons must be a helium atom.

REMEMBER

Everything is made from just over 90 different kinds of atoms.

Elements are substances where all the atoms are of one kind.

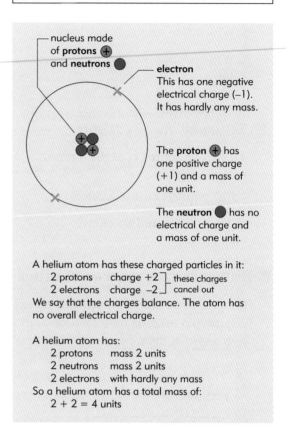

nucleus made of **protons** ⊕ and **neutrons** ●

electron
This has one negative electrical charge (–1). It has hardly any mass.

The **proton** ⊕ has one positive charge (+1) and a mass of one unit.

The **neutron** ● has no electrical charge and a mass of one unit.

A helium atom has these charged particles in it:
2 protons   charge +2 ⎤ these charges
2 electrons   charge –2 ⎦ cancel out
We say that the charges balance. The atom has no overall electrical charge.

A helium atom has:
2 protons   mass 2 units
2 neutrons   mass 2 units
2 electrons   with hardly any mass
So a helium atom has a total mass of:
2 + 2 = 4 units

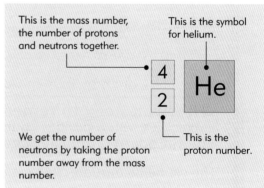

This is the mass number, the number of protons and neutrons together.

This is the symbol for helium.

4
2
He

We get the number of neutrons by taking the proton number away from the mass number.

This is the proton number.

The diagrams show a hydrogen atom and a lithium atom.

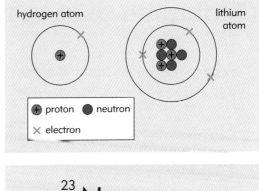

5 Write down the following symbols. Add the mass number and the proton number for each one.

(a) H   (b) Li

6 Copy and complete the following sentence.

A sodium atom has _____ protons

and _____ electrons

and _____ neutrons.

$${}^{23}_{11}\text{Na}$$ a sodium atom

Three kinds of carbon

All carbon atoms contain 6 protons, so they have a proton number of 6.

Carbon atoms can have different numbers of neutrons. This gives the atoms different masses. Atoms of the same element that have different masses are called **isotopes**.

7 Copy and complete the table. The first row has been filled in for you.

Mass number of carbon isotope	Number of protons	Number of neutrons
12	6	6

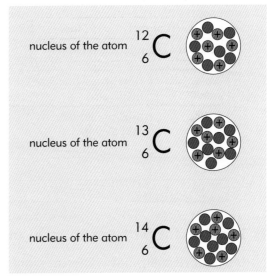

Three isotopes of the element carbon.

<table>
<tr><td colspan="2">What you need to remember [Copy and complete using the key words]</td></tr>
<tr><td colspan="2">

What are atoms made of?

The centre of an atom is called the _____. This can contain two kinds of particle:
- particles with a positive charge called _____
- particles with no charge called _____

Atoms of the same element always have the same number of protons. So every element has its own special _____ number.

The total number of protons and neutrons is called the _____ number.

Atoms of the same element that have different numbers of neutrons are called

_____.

Around the nucleus there are particles with a negative charge called _____.

</td></tr>
</table>

Structure and bonding

12

Making a map of the chemical elements

You already know about two families of elements – the alkali metals and the halogens. There is another family of elements we call the **noble gases**.

What are noble gases like?

The noble gases aren't very interesting. They are colourless so you cannot see them. You cannot use them to make new substances, because they are **unreactive**.

The atoms of the noble gases stay by themselves. They don't even join up to form molecules as other gases do. Even so, there are some uses for the noble gases.

1 Copy and complete the table.

Name of noble gas	How we use the noble gas	Why we can use the gas like this
helium	used to fill balloons and airships	helium is lighter than air and does not burn

Looking for patterns in a list of elements

Different elements have different numbers of **protons** in their atoms.

For example, all hydrogen atoms have 1 proton, all helium atoms have 2 protons.

You can arrange elements in the order of their proton numbers.

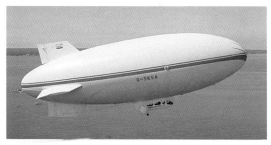

Helium is lighter than air. It is safe because it is non-flammable (does not burn).

A tube filled with neon glows red when electricity is passed through it.

Argon won't react with the metal filament in a lamp, even when it is white hot.

1H 2He 3Li 4Be 5B 6C 7N 8O 9F 10Ne 11Na 12Mg 13Al 14Si 15P 16S 17Cl 18Ar 19K 20Ca

◯ halogen   ◯ alkali metal   ◯ noble gas

2 Look carefully at the list of elements.

(a) What kind of element comes straight after each noble gas?

(b) What kind of element usually comes just before each noble gas?

(c) How many elements must you count before you reach the next one in the same family?

Structure and bonding

The Periodic Table

There is a better way to write all the elements. Instead of using a long line, we start a new line with each new alkali metal. This puts all the elements in a single family in the same column. This gives us the **Periodic Table of the elements**. We call each column a **Group** of the Periodic Table.

3 Copy and complete the following sentences.

The elements in Group 1 belong to the family of

_____ _____ .

The elements in Group 7 belong to the family of

_____ .

The elements in **Group 0** belong to the family of

_____ _____ .

4 In which Group can you find these elements:

beryllium, Be ; magnesium, Mg ; calcium Ca ?

Hydrogen doesn't really belong to any family. We write it on its own in the Periodic Table.

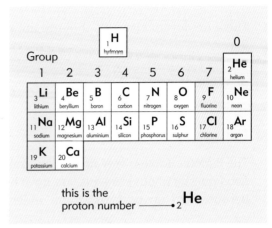

A section of the Periodic Table. A complete version of the Table, containing all the natural elements, is on page 114.

The masses of atoms

The complete Periodic Table usually shows us the mass number and the proton number of each atom.

5 (a) What is the mass number of phosphorus?

(b) What is the proton number of nitrogen?

So far, our Periodic Table contains only the first 20 elements. We need to continue it to include all the others.

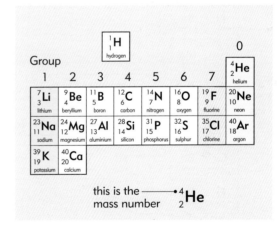

What you need to remember [Copy and complete using the **key words**]

Making a map of the chemical elements

Helium, neon and argon belong to the family of _____ _____ .
These gases are chemically _____ .
In the _____ Table the elements are arranged:
■ in order of how many _____ they have in their atoms
■ so that elements in the same family are in the same column, called a _____ .
The noble gases are in **Group** _____ of the Periodic Table.

113

13

The Periodic Table of all the elements

The complete Periodic Table shows all the elements that we know about. This makes it look more complicated.

There are lots of elements that are not placed in Groups 0 to 7.

1 What do we call these elements?

▨ Using the Periodic Table

The Periodic Table is very useful. You can use it to make good guesses about elements you have never seen. This is because there are patterns we can understand in the Table.

Elements in the same Group are very much alike. If you know the Group in which an element is found, you know some things about the element.

<table>
<tr><td>REMEMBER</td></tr>
</table>

REMEMBER

- the noble gases are in Group 0 of the Periodic Table; they are colourless and unreactive

- the alkali metals are in Group 1 of the Periodic Table; they are soft and reactive

- this is the mass number ^{20}Ne
  this is the proton number $_{10}$

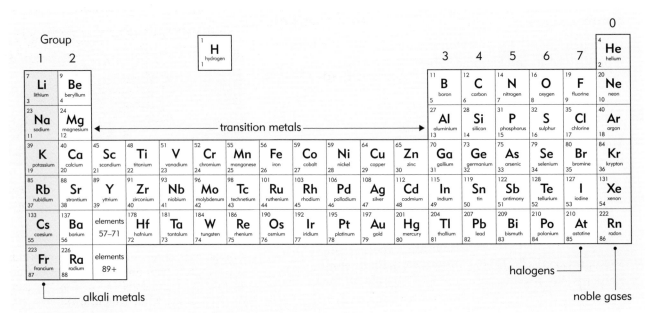

2 (a) In which Group is the element krypton (Kr)?

(b) What do you already know about the elements in this Group?

(c) What can you work out from this about krypton?

3 (a) In which Group is the element caesium?

(b) What do you already know about the elements in this Group?

(c) What can you work out from this about the element caesium?

Structure and bonding

Metals and non-metals in the Periodic Table

This picture of the Periodic Table shows where you can find metals and non-metals.

Group																	0
1	2						H					3	4	5	6	7	He
Li	Be											B	C	N	O	F	Ne
Na	Mg											Al	Si	P	S	Cl	Ar
K	Ca	Sc	Ti	V	Cr	Mn	Fe	Co	Ni	Cu	Zn	Ga	Ge	As	Se	Br	Kr
Rb	Sr	Y	Zr	Nb	Mo	Tc	Ru	Rh	Pd	Ag	Cd	In	Sn	Sb	Te	I	Xe
Cs	Ba	57–71	Hf	Ta	W	Re	Os	Ir	Pt	Au	Hg	Tl	Pb	Bi	Po	At	Rn
Fr	Ra	89+															

☐ metals

▨ non-metals

4 Are the elements in each of these Groups all metals or all non-metals, or does the Group contain both metals and non-metals?

(a) Group 2 (b) Group 7 (c) Group 4

What is special about the transition metals?

Transition metals:

▪ usually have **high** melting points

▪ can often be used to speed up chemical reactions.

Substances that speed up reactions are called **catalysts**.

Look at the pictures of some **compounds** of metals.

5 When you compare the transition metal compounds with the compound of a Group 1 metal, what do you notice?

iron(II) sulphate   iron(III) sulphate   copper sulphate

sodium chloride   copper carbonate

Compounds of transition metal compounds are coloured. **Iron** and **copper** are transition metals. Compounds of Group 1 metals (such as sodium) are white (colourless).

What you need to remember [Copy and complete using the **key words**]

The Periodic Table of all the elements

In the middle of the Periodic Table there is a block of elements we call the _____ metals.

These metals usually have _____ melting points.

They are often used as _____ to speed up chemical reactions.

The _____ of transition metals often have bright colours.

Two commonly used transition metals are _____ and _____.

14

How the Periodic Table was discovered

The story of the Periodic Table tells us a lot about how scientists find things out.

By 1850, scientists knew:

■ that everything is made from the atoms of a small number of elements;

■ how heavy the atoms of different elements are compared to each other (we call this their relative atomic mass);

■ that there are Groups of elements that have similar properties.

1 Write down the names of two Groups of elements.

2 Scientists put the elements calcium and magnesium into the same Group. Explain why.

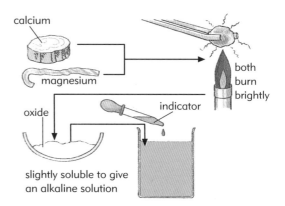

calcium

magnesium

both burn brightly

oxide

indicator

slightly soluble to give an alkaline solution

■ The first periodic table

In 1864, an English scientist called John Newlands wrote down the elements in order, starting with the lightest atoms. He only wrote down the elements he knew about at the time.

He noticed that if you count along seven from any element you reach another similar element. So he wrote down the elements in rows of seven.

This was the first periodic table.

3 Write down three differences between Newlands' periodic table and the Periodic Table that we use today (for the first twenty elements only).

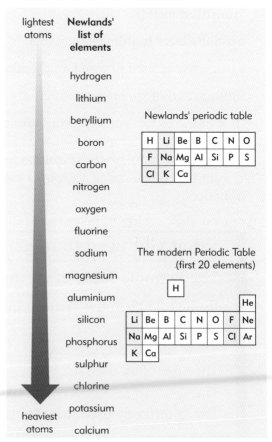

lightest atoms

Newlands' list of elements

hydrogen

lithium

beryllium

boron

carbon

nitrogen

oxygen

fluorine

sodium

magnesium

aluminium

silicon

phosphorus

sulphur

chlorine

potassium

heaviest atoms   calcium

Newlands' periodic table

H	Li	Be	B	C	N	O
F	Na	Mg	Al	Si	P	S
Cl	K	Ca				

The modern Periodic Table (first 20 elements)

■ Improving the idea

Newlands' way of making a periodic table worked fine for the lighter elements. But it didn't work for heavier elements.

Structure and bonding

A Russian scientist called Dmitri Mendeleev found a way to include all the elements he knew about. He did this:

■ by putting any elements that didn't fit the table into a 'dustbin' column (he put many of the elements we call transition metals into this column);

■ by putting each element into the group where it fitted best, even when this meant leaving some blank spaces in his table.

Mendeleev didn't worry about the blank spaces. He just said that there must be some elements which hadn't been discovered yet.

4 Look at the diagram.

(a) Where was there an element missing in Mendeleev's periodic table?

(b) What did Mendeleev expect this element to be like?

(c) Was Mendeleev right about this element?

Mendeleev's periodic table helped scientists to discover many new elements.

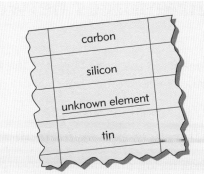

What Mendeleev said the unknown element would be like (in 1869)

• a grey metal
• its oxide would be white
• its chloride:
    would boil at less than 100°C
    each cm³ would weigh 1.9g

The element germanium (discovered 27 years later)

• a grey metal
• a white oxide
• its chloride:
    boils at 86.5°C
    each cm³ weighs 1.8 g

▦ A problem with a noble gas

Mendeleev put the elements in the order of their masses, starting with the lightest element. When some new elements called noble gases were discovered, it was very easy to add a new Group to the Periodic Table. But argon wasn't in quite the right place.

5 Where <u>should</u> argon have gone in the Periodic Table?

Give a reason for your answer.

We now put the elements into the Periodic Table in the order of their <u>proton numbers</u>. The proton number also tells you the number of electrons in each atom. The number of electrons is what gives an element its properties.

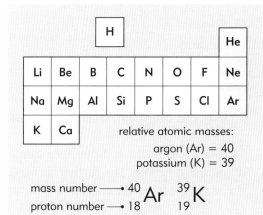

relative atomic masses:

argon (Ar) = 40
potassium (K) = 39

mass number ⟶ $^{40}_{18}$Ar $^{39}_{19}$K
proton number ⟶

What you need to remember

How the Periodic Table was discovered

You should be able to:
■ describe the ideas of Newlands and Mendeleev;
■ explain how these ideas led to the modern Periodic Table.

15

Differences between elements in the same Group

Elements in the same Group of the Periodic Table are similar to each other, but they are not exactly the same.

▇ Differences between alkali metals

Alkali metals all react with water to produce the same kinds of products. Even so, there are some differences in how they each react.

Look at the pictures of three alkali metals reacting with water.

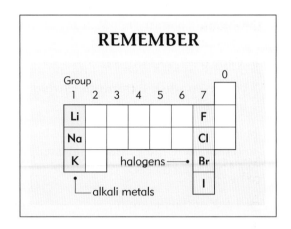

REMEMBER

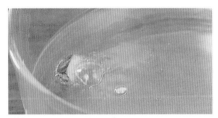

Lithium floats and bubbles.
Hydrogen gas forms.
The water becomes alkaline.

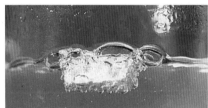

Sodium floats and gets so hot it melts.
Hydrogen gas forms rapidly.
The water becomes alkaline.

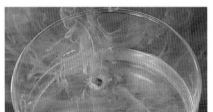

Potassium floats. It reacts violently.
The hydrogen gas burns.
The water becomes alkaline.

1 Write down <u>two</u> ways in which all these reactions are the same.

2 Write down <u>one</u> way in which they are different.

3 Put the three metals in order to show how reactive they are. Start with the one that reacts most quickly.

We say that there is a pattern, or trend, in the way the alkali metals react. The further down Group 1 you go, the more **reactive** the metals are.

The information table shows the **melting points** and **boiling points** of some elements.

4 Copy and complete this table for the alkali metals, using the figures from the information table.

Element	Melting point in °C	Boiling point in °C
lithium		
sodium		
potassium		

5 What is the trend in melting points and boiling points as you go further down Group 1?

Element	Melting point in °C	Boiling point in °C
bromine	−7	59
calcium	840	1484
chlorine	−101	−35
copper	1084	2570
iodine	114	184
lithium	180	1340
magnesium	650	1110
potassium	63	760
sodium	98	880
zinc	420	907

Structure and bonding

Trends in the halogens

The halogens are the elements in Group 7 of the Periodic Table. The halogens also show trends as you go **down** the Group.

Element	Melting point in °C	Boiling point in °C
chlorine		
bromine		
iodine		

6 Copy and complete the table.

7 What happens to the melting points and boiling points as you go down Group 7?

Some halogens are more reactive than others

One halogen can sometimes push a different halogen out of its compound. Here is an example.

chlorine + potassium iodide ⟶ iodine + potassium chloride

We say that in this reaction chlorine **displaces** iodine. Chlorine pushes iodine out of its compound, potassium iodide. This happens because chlorine is more **reactive** than iodine.

The diagrams show two more displacement reactions.

8 Write down the word equation for each reaction.

9 Copy and complete the following sentences.

The reactions show that:

▪ _____ is more reactive than bromine

▪ bromine is more reactive than _____.

As you go down Group 7, the halogens become _____ reactive.

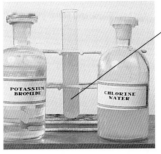

Chlorine displaces bromine from a solution of potassium bromide. The solution goes yellow.

bromine + solution of potassium chloride

iodine + solution of potassium bromide

Bromine displaces iodine from a solution of potassium iodide. The solution goes brown.

most reactive

chlorine

bromine

iodine

least reactive

What we learn from displacement reactions.

What you need to remember [Copy and complete using the **key words**]

Differences between elements in the same Group

The further down Group 1 you go:
▪ the lower the _____ **points** and the _____ **points** are, and
▪ the more _____ the metals are.
The further _____ Group 7 you go:
▪ the higher the melting points and boiling points are, and
▪ the halogens become less _____.
A more reactive halogen _____ a less reactive halogen from its compounds.

Structure and bonding

16

Why are there families of elements?

What elements are like and the way they react depends on the electrons in their atoms. The proton number of an atom tells you how many protons there are in the nucleus. It also tells you how many electrons there are around the nucleus, because the number of protons in an atom is the same as the number of electrons.

1 How many electrons are there in:

(a) a lithium atom

(b) a sodium atom

(c) a potassium atom?

These alkali metals have different numbers of electrons, but the metals still react in a similar way. This is because the electrons are arranged in a similar way.

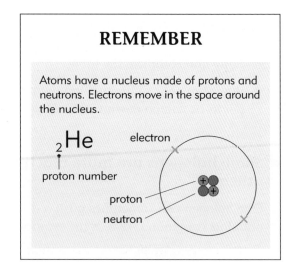

REMEMBER

Atoms have a nucleus made of protons and neutrons. Electrons move in the space around the nucleus.

$_2$He electron

proton number

proton

neutron

Lithium	Sodium	Potassium
$_3$Li	$_{11}$Na	$_{19}$K

Some alkali metals.

How are electrons arranged in an atom?

The electrons around the nucleus of an atom are in certain **energy levels**. The diagram shows the first three energy levels for electrons.

2 Copy and complete this table.

Energy level	Number of electrons that can fit into this level
first (lowest energy)	
second	
third	

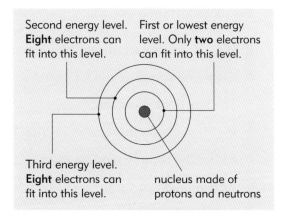

Second energy level. **Eight** electrons can fit into this level.

First or lowest energy level. Only **two** electrons can fit into this level.

Third energy level. **Eight** electrons can fit into this level.

nucleus made of protons and neutrons

How electrons fill up the energy levels

The first energy level is the **lowest**. The electrons start to fill up this level first. When the first energy level is full, electrons start to fill up the second level.

The diagrams show where the electrons are in the first three elements.

3 Draw the same kind of diagram for:

(a) a carbon atom $_6$C

(b) an oxygen atom $_8$O

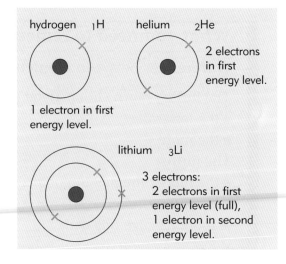

hydrogen $_1$H   helium $_2$He

2 electrons in first energy level.

1 electron in first energy level.

lithium $_3$Li

3 electrons: 2 electrons in first energy level (full), 1 electron in second energy level.

Structure and bonding

Why alkali metals are in the same family

Lithium, sodium and potassium are very similar elements. We call them alkali metals and put them in Group 1 of the Periodic Table.

The diagrams show why these elements are similar. The **top** energy level is the one on the outside of the atom.

4 Copy and complete the following sentences.

The elements in Group 1 are similar to each other. This is because they all have just _____ electron in their top energy level.

A simple way to show electrons

Drawing electron diagrams takes time. Here is a quicker way to show how electrons are arranged in atoms.

sodium $_{11}$Na is   2, 8, 1

2 electrons in lowest energy level which is full   eight electrons in second level which is full   one electron in top energy level

5 Write down the electron arrangement for potassium.

Other families of elements

Elements in the same Group always have the same number of electrons in their top energy levels.

6 Look at the diagram. Copy and complete the table.

Family	Group in the Periodic Table	Number of electrons in top energy level
alkali metals		
halogens		

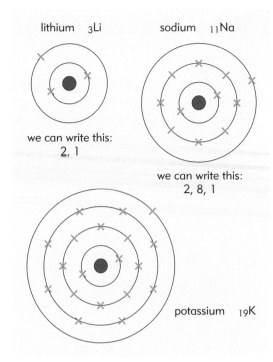

lithium $_3$Li   sodium $_{11}$Na

we can write this:
2, 1

we can write this:
2, 8, 1

potassium $_{19}$K

These show the arrangement of electrons in the alkali metals of Group 1.

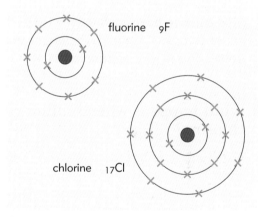

fluorine $_9$F

chlorine $_{17}$Cl

Electrons in Group 7 (halogen) atoms.

What you need to remember [Copy and complete using the **key words**]

Why are there families of elements?

In atoms the electrons are arranged in certain _____ **levels**. The first level has the _____ energy. The lowest level can take up to _____ electrons. The second and third energy levels can each take up to _____ electrons. Elements in the same Group have the same number of electrons in their _____ energy level.

[You should be able to show how the electrons are arranged in the first 20 elements of the Periodic Table.]

Structure and bonding

17

Why elements react to form compounds

Atoms of different elements react together to form compounds. For example, sodium reacts with chlorine to produce the compound sodium chloride.

Elements react because of the electrons in their atoms. The diagrams show the electrons in a sodium atom and in a chlorine atom.

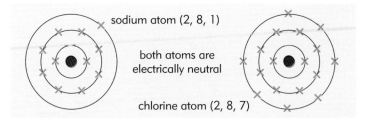

sodium atom (2, 8, 1)

both atoms are electrically neutral

chlorine atom (2, 8, 7)

1 How many electrons are there in the top energy level of

(a) a sodium atom?

(b) a chlorine atom?

Atoms like to have each energy level either completely full or completely empty. The atoms are then more stable. This is why sodium reacts with chlorine.

▨ What happens when sodium reacts with chlorine?

A sodium atom has just 1 electron in the top energy level. The easiest way to become stable is to lose this single electron. The next energy level is now the top one, and is completely full.

A chlorine atom has 7 electrons in its top energy level. The easiest way to become stable is to find 1 more electron. This makes the top energy level completely full.

The diagrams show what happens when sodium reacts with chlorine.

2 Copy and complete the following sentences.

The sodium atom gives the _____ in its top energy level to the _____ atom.

Both atoms now have an electrical _____.

We call Na^+ a sodium _____. We call Cl^- a _____ ion.

REMEMBER

Atoms have electrons in different energy levels around the nucleus. The top energy level is the level on the outside of an atom. There is room for:

2 electrons in the first energy level

8 electrons in the second energy level

8 electrons in the third energy level

The number of electrons in an atom is the same as the number of protons. The proton number tells us how many protons are in the nucleus.

Electrons have a charge of –1.

Protons have a charge of +1.

Atoms have no charge overall because there are equal numbers of protons and electrons in each atom.

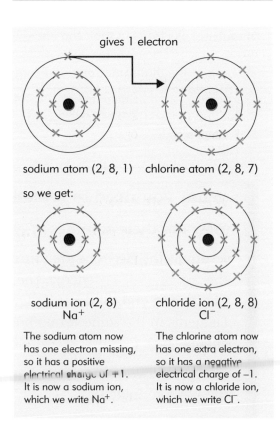

gives 1 electron

sodium atom (2, 8, 1)   chlorine atom (2, 8, 7)

so we get:

sodium ion (2, 8)
Na^+

chloride ion (2, 8, 8)
Cl^-

The sodium atom now has one electron missing, so it has a positive electrical charge of +1. It is now a sodium ion, which we write Na^+.

The chlorine atom now has one extra electron, so it has a negative electrical charge of –1. It is now a chloride ion, which we write Cl^-.

3 Copy the diagram of a lithium atom and a fluorine atom. Then add an arrow to show how the electron moves when they react together.

Substances made from **ions** are called **ionic** substances.

Some more ionic substances

When a metal reacts with a non-metal we get an ionic substance. The metal atoms give away **electrons**. They form **positive** ions. The non-metals take electrons. They form **negative** ions. The diagrams show two examples.

4 Copy the table. Complete it for all the ions shown in the diagrams. The first one is done for you.

Name of ion	Symbol for the ion
magnesium	Mg^{2+}

5 Draw diagrams to show how sodium oxide is formed.

The formula of an ionic substance

Sodium chloride has 1 chloride ion for each sodium ion. We write its formula as NaCl. In calcium chloride there are 2 chloride ions for each calcium ion. We write its formula as $CaCl_2$.

6 Write down the formula for magnesium oxide.

7 Sodium oxide has two Na^+ ions for every one O^{2-} ion. Write down the formula of sodium oxide.

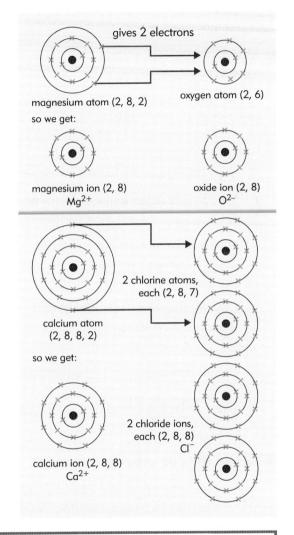

fluorine atom (2, 7)
F

lithium atom (2, 1)
Li

gives 2 electrons

magnesium atom (2, 8, 2)

oxygen atom (2, 6)

so we get:

magnesium ion (2, 8)
Mg^{2+}

oxide ion (2, 8)
O^{2-}

2 chlorine atoms, each (2, 8, 7)

calcium atom (2, 8, 8, 2)

so we get:

2 chloride ions, each (2, 8, 8)
Cl^-

calcium ion (2, 8, 8)
Ca^{2+}

What you need to remember [Copy and complete using the **key words**]

Why elements react to form compounds

When a metal reacts with a non-metal, the metal atoms always give away
_____. They form ions that have a _____ charge.
The non-metal atoms take electrons. They form _____ that have a
_____ charge.
The substances produced are called _____ substances.

[You should be able to show the arrangements of electrons in the ions for sodium chloride, magnesium oxide and calcium chloride.]

Structure and bonding

18

How atoms of non-metals can join together

A non-metal such as chlorine can react with a metal such as sodium. This produces an ionic compound called sodium chloride. Chlorine can also react with another non-metal such as hydrogen.

▥ What happens when chlorine and hydrogen react?

When two non-metals such as chlorine and hydrogen react, they do it by **sharing** electrons. The diagram shows what happens to the shared electrons.

1 Copy and complete the following sentences.

A hydrogen atom and a chlorine atom share one pair of _____. Each atom is then more stable.

The hydrogen atom has a total of _____ electrons in its first energy level. This level is now _____.

The chlorine atom has a total of _____ electrons in its third energy level. This level is also _____.

This makes a _____ of hydrogen chloride.

2 Write down the formula of hydrogen chloride.

▥ Molecules of other substances

Molecular substances are substances that are made of molecules, like hydrogen chloride. Atoms of different non-metals can join together to make molecules. Atoms of the <u>same</u> non-metal element can also share electrons to make molecules.

The diagrams show some molecules of each type.

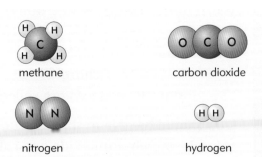

oxygen   water   methane   carbon dioxide

ammonia   chlorine   nitrogen   hydrogen

> **REMEMBER**
>
> We say atoms are stable when each energy level is either completely full of electrons or completely empty.
>
> Atoms with partly full or partly empty energy levels can become more stable if they join up with other atoms.

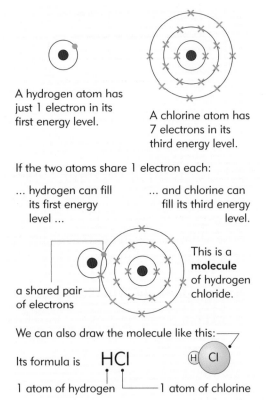

A hydrogen atom has just 1 electron in its first energy level.

A chlorine atom has 7 electrons in its third energy level.

If the two atoms share 1 electron each:

... hydrogen can fill its first energy level ...

... and chlorine can fill its third energy level.

a shared pair of electrons

This is a **molecule** of hydrogen chloride.

We can also draw the molecule like this:

Its formula is   HCl

1 atom of hydrogen   1 atom of chlorine

3 Copy and complete these two tables. The box shows the formula for each molecule in the diagram at the bottom of page 124.

The first row in each table has been filled in for you.

(a)

Name of element	Formula of molecule
oxygen	O_2

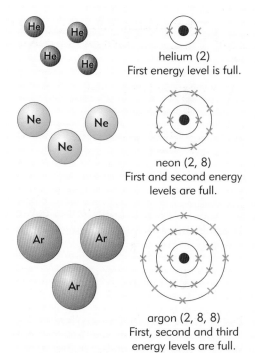

You can also use a formula to show the atoms in a molecule

CH_4 Cl_2 CO_2

H_2 H_2O

N_2 NH_3 O_2

(b)

Name of compound	Formula of molecule
water	H_2O

Atoms that don't join together

Atoms of the noble gases don't usually join with atoms of other elements. Noble gas atoms don't even join up with each other to make molecules.

Look at the way the electrons are arranged in helium, neon and argon atoms. They are all noble gases.

4 Why don't these noble gas atoms give, take or share electrons?

The atoms of noble gases are very stable.

helium (2)
First energy level is full.

neon (2, 8)
First and second energy levels are full.

argon (2, 8, 8)
First, second and third energy levels are full.

Atoms of noble gases don't join up to form molecules.

What you need to remember [Copy and complete using the **key words**]

How atoms of non-metals can join together

Atoms of non-metal elements can join by _____ electrons.

When atoms join together in this way they form a _____.

Substances made of molecules are called _____ substances.

[You should know the formula of each molecule on these pages.]

19 Some differences between ionic and molecular substances

The table shows some of the properties of ionic and molecular substances. The diagram shows some tests we can do.

		Melting point in °C	Boiling point in °C
ionic substances	sodium chloride	801	1413
	calcium chloride	782	1600
	magnesium oxide	2852	3600
molecular substances	methane	182	−161
	ammonia	−77	−34
	water	0	100

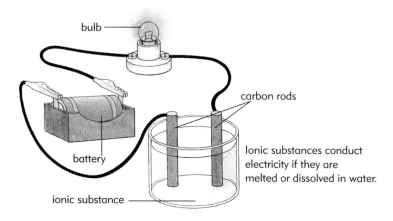

bulb

carbon rods

Ionic substances conduct electricity if they are melted or dissolved in water.

battery

ionic substance

Molecular substances do not conduct electricity.

molecular substance

1 Write down <u>three</u> differences between ionic and molecular substances. Use the information in the table and the diagram to help you.

Why do molecular substances melt so easily?

When a substance melts, the particles inside must break away from the particles on each side.

The diagrams show why this happens more easily in molecular substances.

2 (a) Why do molecular substances have low melting points?

(b) Why do ionic substances have high melting points?

Molecular substances also have **low** boiling points. This is because the weak forces between molecules let them escape more easily into the air as the substance boils.

Methane is made of molecules. There are strong bonds inside each **molecule**, holding the atoms together. The forces **between** separate molecules are only weak.

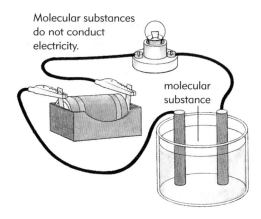

Sodium chloride is an ionic compound. There are strong forces between Na⁺ and Cl⁻ ions. These forces hold the ions together in a **giant** structure. Ionic substances have **high** melting points.

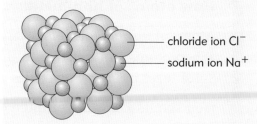

chloride ion Cl⁻

sodium ion Na⁺

Why do ionic substances conduct electricity?

Ionic substances contain particles with electrical charges. A substance will conduct electricity if the charged particles can move about.

3 Why must we melt or dissolve an ionic substance before it will conduct electricity?

4 Why can't molecular substances conduct electricity?

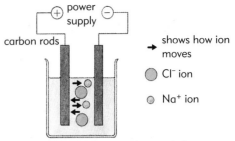

shows how ion moves

Cl^- ion

Na^+ ion

The ions can only move if we melt the substance or dissolve it in water. Molecules do not have electrical charges.

Another kind of giant structure

Atoms can also form giant structures by **sharing** electrons. The diagram shows one example.

5 Would you expect diamond to have a low or a high melting point? Give a reason for your answer.

A diamond is a giant structure of carbon atoms. Each carbon atom shares electrons with the atoms next to it.

All the carbon atoms in a diamond are held together by strong bonds.

Working out the formula of an ionic substance

Ionic substances form giant structures. When ions combine to form compounds, the electrical charges must **balance**. For example, if there are two positive charges, there must also be two negative charges. Look at the examples in the box.

6 Write down the formula for each of these:

(a) potassium bromide   (d) calcium hydroxide

(b) magnesium sulphide   (e) sodium hydroxide

(c) aluminium chloride   (f) aluminium oxide

Na^+ balances	Cl^-	to give the formula NaCl
Ca^{2+} balances {	Cl^- Cl^-	to give the formula $CaCl_2$
Mg^{2+} balances	O^{2-}	to give the formula MgO
Mg^{2+} balances {	OH^- OH^-	to give the formula $Mg(OH)_2$

Some common ions

sodium	Na^+		chloride	Cl^-
potassium	K^+		bromide	Br^-
calcium	Ca^{2+}		hydroxide	OH^-
magnesium	Mg^{2+}		oxide	O^{2-}
aluminium	Al^{3+}		sulphide	S^{2-}

What you need to remember [Copy and complete using the **key words**]

Some differences between ionic and molecular substances

Molecular substances have _____ melting points and boiling points.
This is because there are only weak forces _____ molecules.
There are strong bonds between the atoms inside each _____.
Ionic substances form _____ structures of ions. This is why they have
_____ melting points and boiling points.
Carbon atoms in diamond form a giant structure by _____ electrons.
We should be able to work out the formula of an ionic substance if we are told the charges on each ion. This is because the electrical charges in an ionic substance must
_____.

127

Structure and bonding

Salt – a very useful substance

Ordinary salt is a very important chemical. We use salt for lots of things, and we can make other useful substances from salt.

on food

on icy roads

to preserve food

to make soap

for margarine and plastics

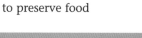

You can get salt by letting seawater evaporate.

1 Write down <u>three</u> different ways to use salt.

2 Write down <u>three</u> materials we can make from salt.

▥ Where do we get the salt we need?

There is a lot of salt dissolved in the **sea**. In some places there are large amounts of salt **underground**. Salt is a cheap raw material because it is easy to collect.

3 How can you get salt from sea water?

4 (a) Where did the underground salt come from?

   (b) How do we usually get salt from under the ground?

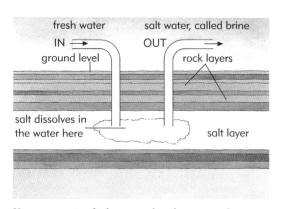
You can get salt from under the ground.

▥ What are the elements in ordinary salt?

The chemical name for ordinary salt is **sodium chloride**.

5 What are the <u>two</u> elements in salt?

6 The two elements by themselves are very different from salt. Write down <u>three</u> differences between salt and the elements sodium and chlorine.

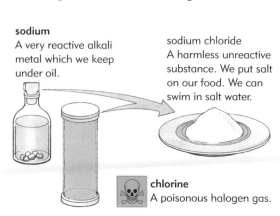
sodium
A very reactive alkali metal which we keep under oil.

sodium chloride
A harmless unreactive substance. We put salt on our food. We can swim in salt water.

chlorine
A poisonous halogen gas.

Structure and bonding

What kind of substance is salt?

The diagram shows the arrangement of the particles in sodium chloride.

7 Copy and complete the following sentences.

Sodium chloride is an _____ substance.
It is made of sodium _____
      and chloride _____.

When we dissolve salt in water, the sodium ions and chloride ions can move about and conduct electricity.

How can we turn salt into other substances?

The diagram shows how we can make other chemicals from salt. We dissolve salt in water to give a solution called **brine**. Next we pass an electric current through the brine. We call this **electrolysis**.

The electrolysis of brine produces three useful substances:

    chlorine gas   **hydrogen** gas
    a solution of the alkali **sodium hydroxide**

8 Copy and complete the table.

Gas	Which electrode produces the gas?	How can you test the gas?
hydrogen		
chlorine		

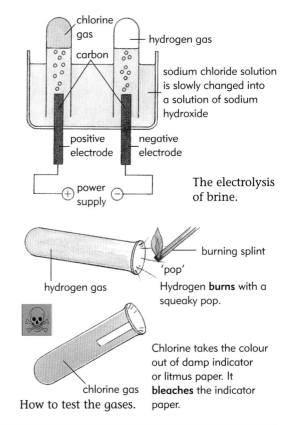

Sodium chloride is an ionic compound.
Na^+ is a sodium ion,
Cl^- is a chloride ion.
The ions are arranged in a regular pattern.

— chloride ion Cl^-
— sodium ion Na^+

chlorine gas
hydrogen gas
carbon
sodium chloride solution is slowly changed into a solution of sodium hydroxide
positive electrode
negative electrode
power supply
The electrolysis of brine.

burning splint
'pop'
hydrogen gas
Hydrogen **burns** with a squeaky pop.

chlorine gas
How to test the gases.
Chlorine takes the colour out of damp indicator or litmus paper. It **bleaches** the indicator paper.

What you need to remember [Copy and complete using the **key words**]

Salt – a very useful substance

The chemical name for salt is _____ _____.
It contains the alkali metal _____ and the halogen _____.
We find salt dissolved in the _____ and buried _____.
A solution of salt in water is called _____.
_____ of brine produces useful new substances.
At the positive electrode we get _____, which _____ damp indicator paper.
At the negative electrode we get _____, which _____ with a squeaky pop.
The solution left at the end contains _____ _____.

21 Using the chemicals we make from salt

How do we use chlorine?

Chlorine is one of the three useful materials we produce from salt water. Chlorine is a poisonous gas. This is useful when we want to kill harmful **bacteria**, but it can also be dangerous.

1 Write down <u>two</u> places where we can kill bacteria with the help of chlorine.

We can use chlorine to make a plastic called **PVC**.

2 (a) Write down <u>two</u> ways in which we can use PVC.

   (b) What do the letters PVC stand for?

You can also make **bleach** from chlorine.

3 (a) What is bleach used for?

   (b) Why is it a bad idea to use bleach with brightly coloured clothes?

Very small amounts of chlorine in water kill dangerous bacteria.

Disinfectants are made from chlorine. They can kill bacteria.

Bleach can be made from chlorine. Bleach removes stains from cloth and makes colours fade.

How do we use hydrogen?

Hydrogen is also made from salt water by electrolysis. Hydrogen is the lightest gas of all, and many years ago airships were filled with hydrogen.

4 Airships filled with hydrogen were very dangerous. Explain why.

We can use hydrogen to make **ammonia**.

5 (a) Which element do we react with hydrogen to make ammonia?

   (b) What useful material is made from ammonia?

Margarine is made using hydrogen.

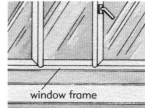

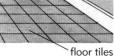

window frame · floor tiles

PVC plastic contains chlorine. PVC is short for poly(vinyl chloride).

+ hydrogen → margarine

vegetable oil

6 What do you react the hydrogen with to make margarine?

Hydrogen gas is flammable. It catches fire very easily.

AMMONIUM NITRATE

Ammonia is made from hydrogen and nitrogen. Ammonia is turned into fertiliser to grow more crops.

Structure and bonding

How do we use sodium hydroxide?

The third material made from salt water is **sodium hydroxide**.

7 (a) Write down <u>one</u> use of sodium hydroxide in the home.

(b) Why should we use safety glasses and gloves when handling sodium hydroxide?

8 Sodium hydroxide is used to make some other useful products. Write down <u>two</u> examples.

Sodium hydroxide is used in oven cleaner. It is corrosive.

Sodium hydroxide attacks and destroys skin and eyes.

Sodium hydroxide helps turn woodpulp into paper.

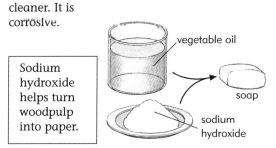

vegetable oil

soap

sodium hydroxide

Making hydrochloric acid

When **hydrogen chloride** gas dissolves in water, we get a solution of hydrochloric **acid**. The equation shows how we can make hydrogen chloride gas. This is a dangerous reaction, which we do not carry out in school.

9 Write down a word equation for this reaction.

10 How can you show that a solution of hydrogen chloride is an acid?

Solutions of hydrogen fluoride, hydrogen bromide and hydrogen iodide are also acidic. These are all hydrogen halides, compounds that are made from hydrogen and the halogen elements (see page 109).

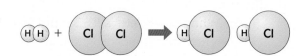

What you need to remember [Copy and complete using the **key words**]

Using the chemicals we make from salt

The three useful materials made by passing electricity through salt water are _____, _____ and sodium hydroxide.

Chlorine is used:
- in substances that kill _____
- to make a plastic called _____
- to make _____, which removes stains and fades colours.

Hydrogen is used:
- to make _____, which can be turned into fertiliser
- to change vegetable oils into _____.

Paper and soap are both made using _____ _____.

Hydrogen reacts with chlorine to make _____ _____.

This dissolves in water to make hydrochloric _____.

The chemicals we use to make photographs

We need special chemicals that react to light to make photographs. These chemicals are placed in layers on a film (or paper) that can be used in a camera. The simplest kind of film produces black and white photographs.

Colour photographs use the same basic chemical reactions, but use lots of other reactions too.

Chemicals that react to light

One of the chemicals we can use to make photographs is silver chloride.
The diagram shows how we can make silver chloride. It also shows what happens when light shines on silver chloride.

1 Complete the word equation for this reaction.

_____ + sodium chloride ⟶ _____ + sodium nitrate

2 (a) What colour is freshly prepared silver chloride?

(b) How does this colour change in the light?

3 Copy and complete the following sentence.

The light changes the white specks of silver chloride into _____ specks of _____ metal.

We say that the light **reduces** the silver chloride to **silver metal**. The same kind of change happens when the other silver **halides** react to light.

4 Write down the names of <u>two</u> other silver halides.

What is photographic film?

The diagram shows what photographic **film** is made from.

5 Copy and complete the following sentence.

Photographic film is made from specks of silver _____ on a _____ plastic sheet.

> **REMEMBER**
>
> Halogens react with metals to form compounds called halides.

This photograph was made using chemicals that are changed by light.

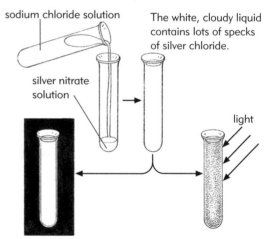

sodium chloride solution

The white, cloudy liquid contains lots of specks of silver chloride.

silver nitrate solution

light

In the dark, the white specks of silver chloride stay white.

In the light, the white specks of silver chloride turn into black specks of silver metal.

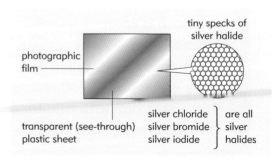

tiny specks of silver halide

photographic film

transparent (see-through) plastic sheet

silver chloride
silver bromide } are all silver halides
silver iodide

Structure and bonding

How does photographic film work?

The diagrams show what happens if you take a photograph of a black cross.

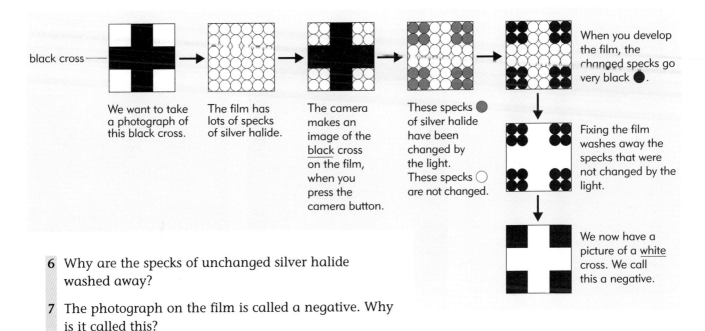

black cross

We want to take a photograph of this black cross.

The film has lots of specks of silver halide.

The camera makes an image of the black cross on the film, when you press the camera button.

These specks ● of silver halide have been changed by the light. These specks ○ are not changed.

When you develop the film, the changed specks go very black ●.

Fixing the film washes away the specks that were not changed by the light.

We now have a picture of a white cross. We call this a negative.

6 Why are the specks of unchanged silver halide washed away?

7 The photograph on the film is called a negative. Why is it called this?

Photographic paper works in the same way.

What else can change silver halides?

X-rays and the radiation from **radioactive** materials will also reduce silver halides.

8 How can X-rays make a photograph of bones inside your body?

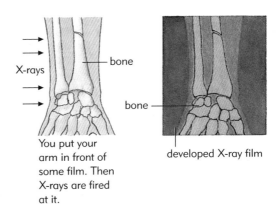

X-rays — bone

You put your arm in front of some film. Then X-rays are fired at it.

bone

developed X-ray film

What you need to remember [Copy and complete using the **key words**]

The chemicals we use to make photographs

Silver chloride, silver bromide and silver iodide are all silver _____ .

Light can change silver halides into _____ **metal**. We say that light _____ silver halides to silver metal.

Silver halides are also reduced by _____ and the radiation from _____ substances.

We use silver halides to make photographic _____ and photographic paper.

1

Using heat to speed things up

Some chemical reactions are very fast, others are slow.
The reactions go at different speeds or **rates**.

The explosion takes a fraction of a second.

The tablet reacts with water in about a minute.

The nail takes a few hours to start rusting. It takes many months to rust completely.

1 Describe <u>one</u> example each of a chemical reaction that is

(a) very slow, which takes hours or days,

(b) very fast, which takes seconds or less,

(c) medium speed, which takes one minute or so.

▨ Speeding up reactions in the kitchen

When we cook food there are chemical reactions going on. How fast the food cooks depends on how hot we make it.

2 Look at the pictures.

(a) Which is faster, cooking in boiling water or in cooking oil?

(b) Why do you think this is?

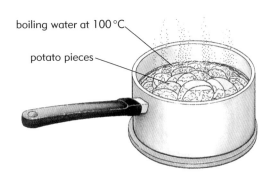

boiling water at 100 °C

potato pieces

The pieces of potato take about 20 minutes to cook.

cooking oil at 130 °C, a **higher** temperature than water

chips

The chips take only a few minutes to cook.

How much difference does temperature make?

Look at the colour change reaction.

3 Copy and complete the following sentences.

The higher the temperature the _____ the time the reaction takes.
This means that the rate of reaction is _____.

4 How long do you think the reaction will take at temperatures of

(a) 60 °C   (b) 10 °C?

Using temperatures to control reactions

If you increase the temperature by 10°C, chemical reactions go about twice as fast. To **slow down** a chemical reaction you must reduce the temperature.

5 Where can you put milk to slow down the chemical reactions that make it go bad?

6 About how long will it take the milk to go sour in the fridge?

7 (a) How many times faster do the potatoes cook in the pressure cooker?

(b) What does this tell you about the temperature of the water inside the pressure cooker?

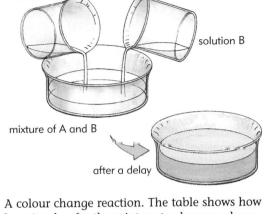

solution A

solution B

mixture of A and B

after a delay

A colour change reaction. The table shows how long it takes for the mixture to change colour.

Temperature (°C)	20	30	40	50
Time taken to go blue (seconds)	400	200	100	50

Chemical reactions make food go bad.

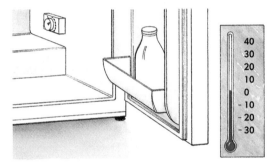

Inside a fridge, the milk takes many days to go sour.

Outside, the milk goes sour in two days.

water boiling at 100 °C

The potatoes take about 24 minutes to cook.

pressure cooker

The potatoes take about 6 minutes to cook.

What you need to remember [Copy and complete using the **key words**]

Using heat to speed things up

Chemical reactions go at different speeds or _____.
Chemical reactions go faster at _____ temperatures.
At low temperatures, chemical reactions _____ _____.

2

Making solutions react faster

Some substances will dissolve in water to make a **solution**. You can use solutions for many chemical reactions. The speed of these chemical reactions depends on how strong the solutions are.

1 What is the chemical solution in a car battery ?

■ 'Strong' and 'weak' solutions

Your friend likes her tea to taste sweet, but not too sweet.

one spoonful — sugar
not sweet enough
sugar solution is too weak

two spoonfuls
just right

three spoonfuls
too sweet
sugar solution is too strong

> **REMEMBER**
>
> A reaction that takes a short time has a high speed or rate.

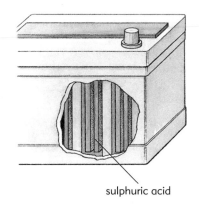

sulphuric acid

The chemical reactions in a car battery need sulphuric acid of just the right strength.

2 Look at the diagrams. Copy and complete the table.

Spoonfuls of sugar	What your friend's tea tasted like	Strength of sugar solution
1		
2		perfect
3		

3 A mug of tea is 1.5 times bigger than one of the cups shown above.
How many spoonfuls of sugar should your friend put into a mug of tea? Give a reason for your answer.

■ Dilute to taste

We call a 'strong' solution a **concentrated** solution. To make a solution 'weaker', we **dilute** it with water.

4 Look at the diagrams.
Copy and complete the following sentences.

The orange drink in the bottle is _____.
To make it good to drink you need to _____ it.

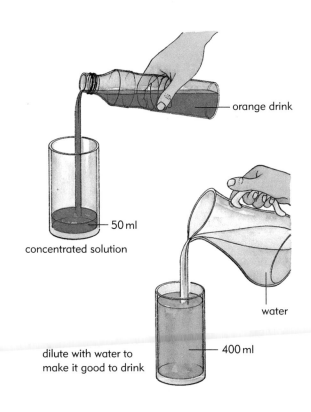

orange drink

concentrated solution — 50 ml

water

dilute with water to make it good to drink — 400 ml

Patterns of chemical change

■ How does concentration affect the speed of a chemical reaction?

Look at the pictures of the reaction between a chemical we call thio and an acid.

5 Copy and complete the following sentences.

The most concentrated solution contains _____ spatulas of thio crystals.

The reaction with the most concentrated thio solution takes the _____ time.

This means that this reaction has the _____ rate.

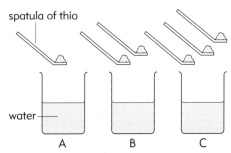

Some students make 3 different strengths of thio solution.

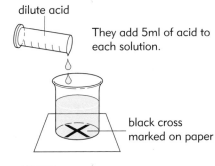

They add 5ml of acid to each solution.

The solution gradually goes cloudy.

■ Making gases react faster

Some gases will react together to make new substances. For example, you can make ammonia gas by reacting together a mixture of nitrogen and hydrogen gases.

You can squeeze gases into a smaller space. This is like making a more concentrated solution. The gases will then react together faster. A **high** pressure gas is like a very concentrated solution.

6 A chemical factory makes ammonia gas. They already make the hydrogen and nitrogen as hot as they can. What else should they do to make the reaction go faster?

Eventually you can't see the cross when looking down through the solution.

Results.

Solution	Time for cross to disappear
A	8 minutes
B	4 minutes
C	2.5 minutes

What you need to remember [Copy and complete using the **key words**]

Making solutions react faster

When you dissolve a substance in water you get a _____.

A solution that contains a lot of dissolved substance is a _____ solution.

To make a concentrated solution react more slowly, you can _____ it.

To make gases react faster, you need a _____ pressure.

Making solids react faster

The diagrams show a chemical reaction between a solid and a solution.

1 Write down

(a) the name of the solid in the reaction

(b) the name of the solution used

(c) the name of the gas produced.

2 Copy and complete the word equation for this reaction.

$$\underline{} + \underline{}\text{ acid} \longrightarrow \underline{}\text{ dioxide} + \underline{}$$

bubbles of carbon dioxide gas

dilute hydrochloric acid

limestone

During the reaction.

solution of calcium chloride

limestone (now smaller)

When all the acid has been used up, the reaction stops.

■ Making the reaction faster

One way to make the reaction faster is by using more concentrated acid. But how fast the limestone reacts also depends on how big the pieces of limestone are.

3 Look at the diagrams.

Copy and complete the table.

Size of solid pieces	Time taken to react	Speed of reaction
one large piece		
several small pieces		
lots of very small pieces		

4 Copy and complete the following sentence.

The smaller the bits of limestone, the _____ they react with the acid.

With one large piece of limestone, the gas bubbles continue for 10 minutes.

100 ml acid

100 ml acid

With smaller pieces, the gas bubbles continue for 1 minute. The bubbling is faster.

100 ml acid

With very small pieces, the gas bubbles continue for a few seconds. The bubbling is very fast.

Patterns of chemical change

Do you suck or crush sweets?

Think about eating a hard sweet. If you suck the sweet in one piece it lasts quite a long time. If you crush the sweet into little pieces it doesn't last so long.

5 Why does the crushed sweet dissolve faster? Explain your answer as fully as you can.

Sucking your sweet. Your saliva can only get at the outside **surface** of the sweet.

— one large piece

Crushing your sweet. Your saliva can get at more of the sweet at once.

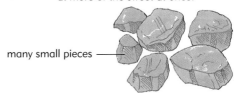

many small pieces —

Why small bits react faster

The same amount of limestone in smaller bits reacts **faster**. The acid can get at smaller bits better. This is because they have more **surface area**.

6 Look at the large cube of limestone.

(a) How many little squares are there on one face of the large cube?

(b) How many faces are there on the cube?

(c) What is the total number of small squares on the surface of the cube? This is the surface area of the cube.

7 Now look at the large cube broken up into smaller cubes.

(a) What is the surface area of each small cube?

(b) What is the total surface area of all the small cubes added together?

(c) How many times more surface area do the small cubes have than the large cube?

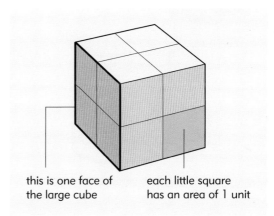

this is one face of the large cube

each little square has an area of 1 unit

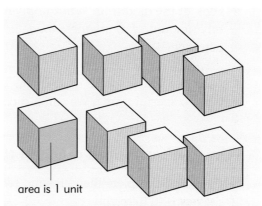

area is 1 unit

What you need to remember [Copy and complete using the **key words**]

Making solids react faster

A solid can react with a liquid only where they touch. The reaction is on the _____ of the solid.

If we break up the solid, we increase the total _____ _____.

This means that smaller pieces react _____.

4

Substances that speed up reactions

People use hydrogen peroxide to bleach hair. It does this by releasing oxygen. The oxygen turns the hair a very pale blonde colour.

stopper

a few gas bubbles

hydrogen peroxide solution

1 Copy and complete the word equation for this reaction

hydrogen peroxide ⟶ _____ + _____

In the bottle, the hydrogen peroxide very slowly splits up into oxygen gas and water.

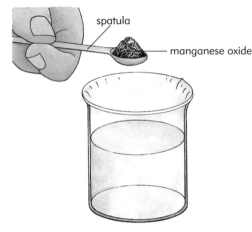

spatula

manganese oxide

hydrogen peroxide solution

The hydrogen peroxide starts to bubble very fast. It splits up.

water

manganese oxide

When all the hydrogen peroxide has split up, the manganese oxide is still there.

2 Look at the diagrams. What happens if you put a tiny amount of manganese oxide into some hydrogen peroxide?

A substance which speeds up a chemical reaction in this way has a special name. We call it a **catalyst**.

■ Why don't you need much of the catalyst?

3 Copy and complete the following sentences using the diagrams to help you.

The _____ _____ is not used up in the chemical reaction. It is still there at the end. You can use it over and over again to split up more _____ _____.

4 How could you collect the catalyst so that you could use it again?

5 How does this experiment show that a catalyst is not used up in the reaction?

You can use the same manganese oxide **over** and **over** again. First filter the water and manganese oxide.

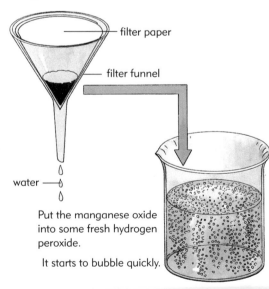

filter paper

filter funnel

water

Put the manganese oxide into some fresh hydrogen peroxide.

It starts to bubble quickly.

Patterns of chemical change

You can show that the catalyst is not one of the ordinary chemicals that react, by writing your equation like this.

$$\text{hydrogen peroxide} \xrightarrow{\text{manganese oxide}} \text{oxygen} + \text{water}$$

We write the name of the catalyst above the arrow.

Sunflower oil is a vegetable oil. This oil can be reacted with hydrogen to make margarine, using nickel as a catalyst.

■ What can we make using catalysts?

We can make lots of useful materials using catalysts. These materials **cost** less to make when you use a catalyst. Usually each chemical reaction needs its own **special** catalyst.

6 What is the catalyst we use to make margarine?

7 What substance do we make using a catalyst called vanadium oxide?

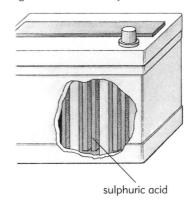

sulphuric acid

■ Why do cars have catalytic converters?

Car batteries contain sulphuric acid. We make this acid using a catalyst called vanadium oxide.

Look at the diagrams.

1

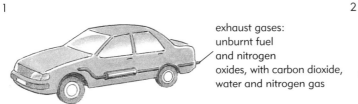

exhaust gases: unburnt fuel and nitrogen oxides, with carbon dioxide, water and nitrogen gas

2

exhaust gases: carbon dioxide, water and nitrogen gas

catalytic converter

The catalytic converter changes harmful gases into safer gases. The catalyst is not **used up** in the reactions.

8 Why do we fit cars with catalytic converters?

9 You often have to fill up a car's fuel tank. You don't have to add more catalyst to the converter. Why is this?

What you need to remember [Copy and complete using the **key words**]

Substances that speed up reactions

A substance that speeds up a chemical reaction is called a _____.

The catalyst increases the rate of reaction but is not _____ _____.

You can use catalysts _____ and _____ again.

Each chemical reaction needs its own _____ catalyst.

Useful materials such as margarine and sulphuric acid _____ less to make when we use catalysts.

Patterns of chemical change

5

Investigating the speed of reactions

Looking and timing

All you need to measure the speed of many chemical reactions is a clock. You can then watch the reaction carefully to see how it changes.

You need to look out for different things in different reactions.

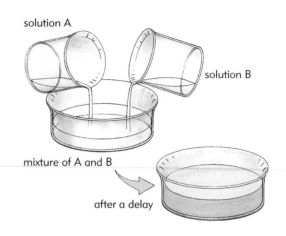

solution A

solution B

mixture of A and B

after a delay

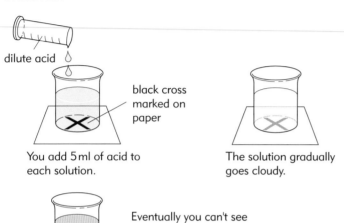

dilute acid

black cross marked on paper

You add 5 ml of acid to each solution.

The solution gradually goes cloudy.

Eventually you can't see the cross when looking down through the solution.

bubbles of carbon dioxide gas

dilute hydrochloric acid

limestone

During the reaction.

1 Write down <u>three</u> different things you might look for when you are timing a chemical reaction.

How much gas is produced?

Some chemical reactions produce a gas.

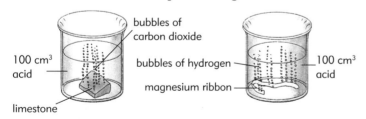

bubbles of carbon dioxide

100 cm³ acid

bubbles of hydrogen

magnesium ribbon

100 cm³ acid

limestone

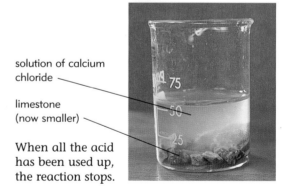

solution of calcium chloride

limestone (now smaller)

When all the acid has been used up, the reaction stops.

2 Write down the name of the gas produced when

(a) limestone reacts with acid

(b) magnesium reacts with acid.

You can collect the gas and measure how much there is. Then you can use your results to draw a graph.

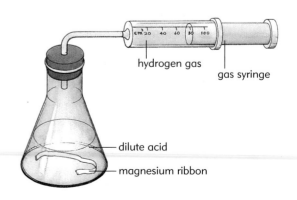

hydrogen gas

gas syringe

dilute acid

magnesium ribbon

3 How can you collect and measure a gas produced during a reaction?

Patterns of chemical change

Look at the graph. It shows the results of the experiment of magnesium reacting with acid. A gas syringe was used to collect the gas.

4 Copy and complete the following sentences.

During the first two minutes the reaction is

_____.

Then for the next two minutes the reaction is

_____ _____.

After four minutes the reaction is _____, and no more _____ is produced.

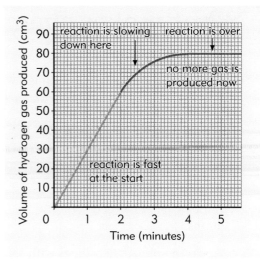

How does the mass change?

You can also measure the rate of reaction by weighing. If a gas escapes into the air during a reaction, the mass of what is left goes down.

The graphs show some students' results for this experiment.

5 Look at the graphs.

(a) Which reaction takes longer to finish?

(b) Which reaction has the faster rate?

(c) How much carbon dioxide gas is produced in each reaction?

6 Why is there a cotton wool plug in the neck of the flask?

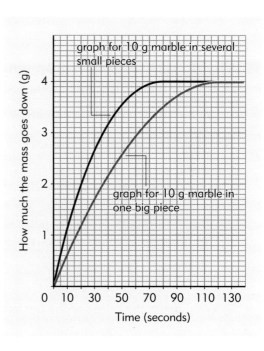

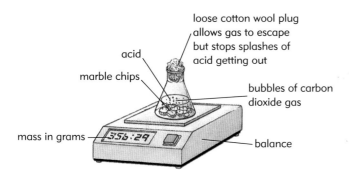

What you need to remember

Investigating the speed of reactions

You may be given some similar information to the examples given above.

You must be able to explain what the information tells you about the rate of reactions.

Patterns of chemical change

6

What makes chemical reactions happen?

Chemical reactions can only happen when the particles of different substances **collide** with each other.

The diagram shows what happens when carbon burns in oxygen.

1 Copy and complete the sentences.

A molecule of oxygen contains _____ oxygen atoms.

When the molecule collides with some hot carbon, the oxygen atoms join with a _____ atom to make a molecule of _____ _____.

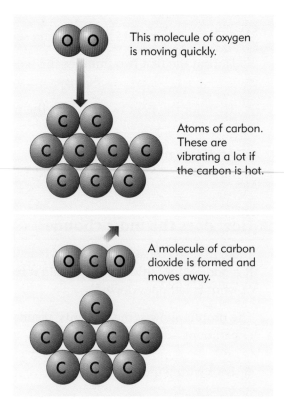

This molecule of oxygen is moving quickly.

Atoms of carbon. These are vibrating a lot if the carbon is hot.

A molecule of carbon dioxide is formed and moves away.

▦ Why do reactions speed up when you increase the temperature?

The higher the temperature, the **faster** the oxygen molecules move.

2 Write down <u>two</u> reasons why faster-moving oxygen molecules react more easily with carbon.

The smallest amount of energy particles must have for a reaction to occur is called the **activation** energy.

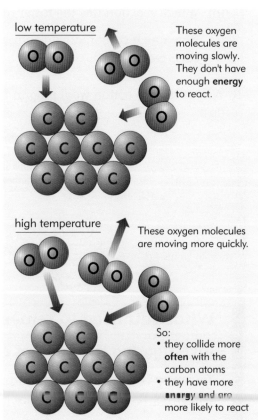

low temperature

These oxygen molecules are moving slowly. They don't have enough **energy** to react.

high temperature

These oxygen molecules are moving more quickly.

So:
• they collide more **often** with the carbon atoms
• they have more **energy** and are more likely to react

Why does breaking up a solid make it react faster?

A lump of iron doesn't react very quickly with oxygen, even if it is very hot. But the tiny specks of iron in a sparkler burn quite easily.

3 Why do tiny specks of iron react more easily than a big lump of iron?

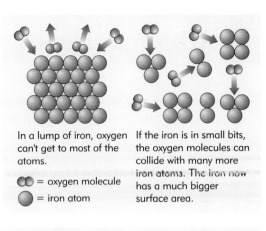

In a lump of iron, oxygen can't get to most of the atoms.

If the iron is in small bits, the oxygen molecules can collide with many more iron atoms. The iron now has a much bigger surface area.

⬤⬤ = oxygen molecule

⬤ = iron atom

Why do strong solutions react faster?

Magnesium metal reacts with acid.

The reaction is faster if the acid is made more concentrated.

4 Explain why the reaction is faster in more concentrated acid.

○ water molecule   ● particle from acid   ◁▭ magnesium ribbon

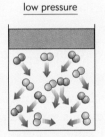 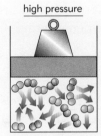

dilute acid

concentrated acid

There are not very many collisions between particles from the acid and the magnesium.

Collisions between particles from the acid and the magnesium happen far more often.

Another way to make gases react faster

Gases react faster if they are hot.

The diagrams show another way to make gases react faster.

low pressure

high pressure

Collisions between different molecules do not happen very often.

Collisions between different molecules are much more **frequent**.

What you need to remember [Copy and complete using the **key words**]

What makes chemical reactions happen?

For substances to react:
- their particles must _____;
- the particles must have enough _____ when they do this.

The smallest amount of energy they need is called the _____ energy.

If you increase the temperature, reactions happen faster. This is because the particles collide more _____ and with more _____.

Breaking solids into smaller pieces, making solutions more concentrated and increasing the pressure of gases all make reactions _____. All these things make the collisions between particles more _____.

Patterns of chemical change

7

Getting energy out of chemicals

On a barbecue you **burn** charcoal to cook the food.
Burning charcoal releases **energy** in the form of **heat**.
Burning charcoal is an example of a chemical reaction.

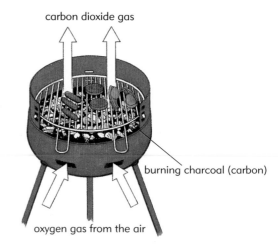

carbon dioxide gas

burning charcoal (carbon)

oxygen gas from the air

1 Copy and complete the word equation for the chemical reaction.

_____ + carbon ⟶ _____ + energy

Substances that we burn to release energy are called **fuels**.

▥ Are all fuels the same?

All fuels release energy as they burn. Different fuels give different waste gases.

If a fuel contains carbon it produces carbon dioxide when it burns.

If a fuel contains hydrogen it produces water vapour when it burns.

Many fossil fuels such as coal and oil contain a little sulphur. If a fuel contains some sulphur, it produces sulphur dioxide gas when it burns.

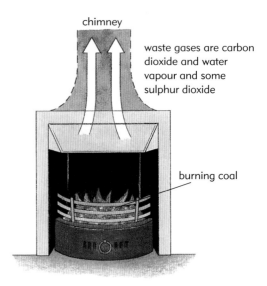

chimney

waste gases are carbon dioxide and water vapour and some sulphur dioxide

burning coal

2 Copy the table. Use the information from the pictures to complete the table.

Name of the fuel	Gases produced when the fuel burns	What the fuel contains
charcoal		
coal		
butane		

3 Copy and complete the word equation for burning some camping gas.

_____ _____ _____
    +   ⟶   +   + energy
  oxygen   _____ _____

waste gases are carbon dioxide and water vapour

burning gas

camping gas cooker

butane gas

What other reactions release energy?

Many chemical reactions happen in solutions.
These reactions may also release some energy.

Look at the diagrams.

4 How do you know that this reaction releases energy?

5 Copy and complete the word equation for this reaction.

thermometer reads 15 °C

thermometer reads 19 °C

some zinc left over

zinc

hydrochloric acid

bubbles of hydrogen gas

solution of zinc chloride

_____ + _____ ⟶ _____ + _____ + ⟨energy⟩

Naming reactions that release energy

Chemical reactions that release energy are called **exothermic** reactions.

6 Copy and complete the following sentences.

'Ex' means _____.

'Therm' means something to do with _____.

So 'exothermic' means _____ going _____.

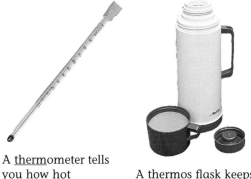

An <u>ex</u>it sign is where you go <u>out</u>.

A <u>therm</u>ometer tells you how <u>hot</u> something is.

A <u>therm</u>os flask keeps the <u>heat</u> in.

Other types of energy released by chemical reactions

Some chemical reactions release different kinds of energy. Look at the diagrams.

7 What other kinds of energy do these chemical reactions release?

A stone quarry.

What you need to remember [Copy and complete using the **key words**]

Getting energy out of chemicals

Charcoal, coal, gas and wood are all _____.
When we _____ them they release energy in the form of _____.
Many other chemical reactions also release _____ into the surroundings.
We call reactions like this _____ reactions.

Patterns of chemical change

8

Do chemical reactions always release energy?

Many chemical reactions release energy.

1 Write down <u>two</u> examples of chemical reactions that release energy.

2 Copy and complete the following sentence.

A reaction that releases heat energy is called an _____ reaction.

Other reactions will happen only if we **supply** energy. We call these **endothermic** reactions.

You have to supply energy to cook the egg.

3 Write down <u>one</u> everyday example of an endothermic reaction.

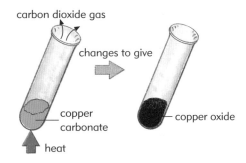

carbon dioxide gas

changes to give

copper carbonate

heat

copper oxide

Using heat to make reactions happen

We can make some chemical reactions happen by supplying energy in the form of **heat**. This is why a Bunsen burner is so useful, it supplies heat energy.

4 Look at the diagrams.

Copy and complete the word equations for the <u>two</u> endothermic reactions.

copper + ⁓energy⁓ ⟶ copper + _____
_____   _____

lead + _____ + ⁓_____⁓ ⟶ _____ + _____
oxide   _____

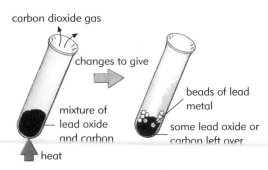

carbon dioxide gas

changes to give

mixture of lead oxide and carbon

heat

beads of lead metal

some lead oxide or carbon left over

■ Using electricity to make reactions happen

We can make some chemical reactions happen by supplying energy in the form of **electricity**.

We can use electricity to obtain copper metal from a solution of copper chloride.

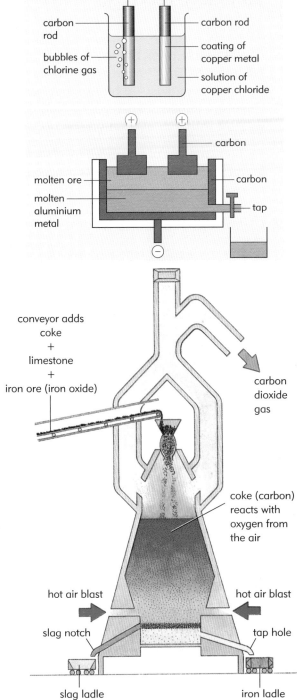

5 Copy and complete the word equation for this reaction.

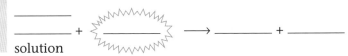

_____ + ⟨energy⟩ ⟶ _____ + _____
solution

■ Extracting metals from their natural ores

You need to supply energy to extract metals from ores.

6 Copy and complete the following sentence.

The chemical reactions we use to extract metals from their ores are _____-thermic reactions.

7 How do you supply the energy you need to extract aluminium from aluminium ore?

8 How do you supply the energy you need to extract iron from iron ore in a blast furnace?

■ Reactions that use light energy

When you take a photograph, **light** energy changes the chemicals in the film. Films contain silver halides. The word equation is:

silver halide + ⟨energy⟩ ⟶ silver metal + halogen

9 Copy and complete the following sentence.

In photography _____ energy changes silver halides into _____ _____ and the halogens.

What you need to remember [Copy and complete using the **key words**]

Do chemical reactions always release energy?

To make some chemical reactions happen you must _____ energy.

We call these reactions _____ reactions.

We must supply energy to extract metals from their ores.

We can supply this energy in the form of _____ or _____.

The chemical reactions in photography use _____ energy.

9

Living things can do our chemistry for us

Lots of people think that chemistry happens only in laboratories. They imagine that chemicals react in strange bits of glass – a bit like in a horror film! But chemistry happens wherever we change the substances we start with into new substances.

So, there are lots of places where chemical reactions happen. One of these places is inside your body.

Chemical reactions in your body

1 Lots of chemical reactions take place in your body all the time. A few of them are shown in the table.

Part of body	Starting material in chemical reaction	New material made in chemical reaction
mouth	starch	sucrose
muscles	glucose	carbon dioxide
gut	sucrose	glucose

(a) Which part of your body turns starch into sucrose?

(b) What new substance do your muscles change glucose into?

(c) Your body makes glucose in your gut. What substance does your gut start with to make glucose from?

Yeast cells are used to make bread.

Yeast cells help us to make beer.

Chemical reactions in other living cells

Chemical reactions take place in the cells of all living things. We can use **living cells** to make chemicals for us.

2 Look at the photographs.

Copy the table below. Then fill it in using the information in the photographs. The first one is done for you.

Type of living cells	What the living cells help us to make
yeast	bread

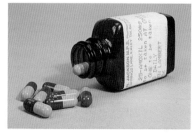

The drug penicillin is made by **moulds**.

Bacteria help us to make yogurt.

Using yeast to make wine

Yeasts are very useful living things. Yeast cells make the chemical called **alcohol** in wine and beer.

3 Look at the photograph of yeast cells under the microscope.

   Copy and complete the word equation.

$$\text{sugar} \xrightarrow{\text{yeast}} \underline{\hspace{2cm}} + \underline{\hspace{2cm}} \underline{\hspace{2cm}}$$

We call this reaction **fermentation**.

4 Look at the picture of wine being made.

   How can you tell that the grape juice is fermenting?

Using yeast to make bread

The **carbon dioxide** that the yeast makes is useful too. This gas helps to make bread rise. When you slice through bread you can see lots of tiny holes.

5 What do you think causes these holes?

6 Look at the diagram on the right. Copy and complete the following sentence.

   You can tell that yeast makes carbon dioxide gas because this gas makes _____ _____ turn milky.

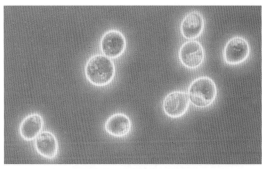

These are yeast cells. When they have plenty of food (**sugar**) they can grow and divide quickly. They turn the sugar into alcohol and the gas carbon dioxide.

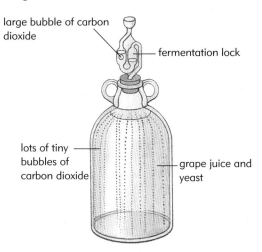

Making wine. The sugar for the reaction comes from the grape juice.

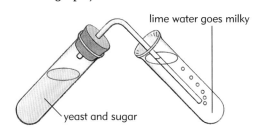

A simple test for carbon dioxide.

What you need to remember [Copy and complete using the **key words**]

Living things can do our chemistry for us

We can use _____ _____ to help us make new substances.

Examples of living things we can use in this way are _____ and _____.

When we make wine and beer, we use yeast cells to turn _____ into _____ . We call this reaction _____.

Yeast also makes the gas called _____ _____. The bubbles of this gas help bread to rise.

10

More cells that will work for us

Bacteria are living cells. Some bacteria can be harmful to us. Other bacteria are very helpful.

1 Look at the photos.

Write down (a) <u>one</u> example of harmful bacteria

(b) <u>one</u> example of helpful bacteria.

REMEMBER

Living cells can make chemicals that are very useful to us.

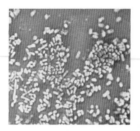
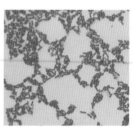

Harmful bacteria that cause the disease cholera.

Helpful bacteria that we use to make yogurt.

▥ Making yogurt

The diagram shows how you can make yogurt.

2 Copy and complete the following sentences.

To turn milk into _____ we need living cells called _____.

They feed on the _____ in the milk and turn it into _____ _____.

3 Where do the bacteria come from to make the next batch of yogurt?

▥ Just the right temperature

Living cells make new substances fastest if they are at just the right temperature. If the cells are too cold then the reactions only happen slowly. If cells are too hot, they can be damaged.

4 Copy and complete the following sentence.

The best temperature for making yogurt is _____.

▥ Why are living things such good chemists?

Living things contain **enzymes**, which help them to make new materials. Enzymes do this by speeding up chemical reactions. Because of enzymes, reactions in cells are quite fast, even though the cells are not very hot.

There are thousands of different enzymes, just as there are thousands of chemical reactions that happen in living things.

yogurt bacteria

milk

Milk contains a **sugar** called lactose.

Yogurt bacteria use up the sugar and make **lactic acid**.

keep in a warm place (about 40 °C) for 12 hours

there are now many more bacteria, so we can use a little of this yogurt to start the next batch

yogurt

The milk turns into yogurt.

Patterns of chemical change

5 What do we call substances (like enzymes) that speed up chemical reactions?

6 Copy and complete the following sentence.

Because of _____, reactions in living cells are quite fast, even though the temperature isn't very

_____.

Why mustn't enzymes be made too hot?

Enzymes are made from **protein**. They are big molecules and they have special shapes that help them to work.

There are proteins in the white of an egg. If you put an egg in hot water the protein **changes**, and you can't change it back again.

A raw egg.

An egg after it has been heated.

7 Why do you think heat damages or destroys enzymes?

Whiter than white

Lots of washing powders contain enzymes. We call them biological washing powders. The enzymes break down the stains on clothes. Biological washing powders are good at removing biological stains like blood and egg.

It is important to use the powders at the correct temperature.

8 Look at the table.

(a) At which temperature is 'Cleeno' best at removing blood stains? Why is this?

(b) 'Cleeno' can't remove blood stains at all at 55 °C. Why not?

Temperature of wash in °C	What happened to blood stain
15	
25	
35	
45	
55	

What you need to remember [Copy and complete using the **key words**]

More cells that will work for us

The type of living cells that make yogurt are called _____.
They feed on the _____ in the milk and turn it into _____

_____.

To speed up their chemical reactions, living cells contain _____.
These need to be warm to work well, but must not get too hot as they are made from

_____.

Protein _____ when it is heated and cannot be changed back again.

11

Not too hot and not too cold

What makes food go bad?

Food will not stay fresh for ever, sooner or later it starts to break down or go bad. This is because **living cells** start to feed on it.

Bacteria are breaking down this cheese.

This rotting fruit is covered in mould.

Yeast is making this peach go soft.

1 Look at the photographs. Give the names of <u>three</u> types of living cells that help to make the food go bad.

In a warm room, living cells like bacteria grow and multiply quickly. This means that they can break down food quite fast.

2 Why can bacteria break down food quickly in a warm room?

3 The temperature in our bodies is 37 °C. This temperature is ideal for any bacteria that get inside us. Explain why.

Keeping food fresh

To stop food from going bad we often keep it in a **fridge** or a **freezer**. The diagrams tell you why this works.

4 Copy and complete the table.

	Temperature	How well enzymes work	How long food stays fresh
fridge			
freezer			

3 °C

In the fridge, living cells can only break down food slowly. Their **enzymes** do not work well at this **low** temperature. Food stays fresh for several days.

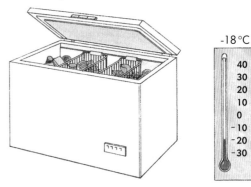

-18 °C

In the freezer, living cells cannot break down food at all. Their enzymes do not work at this very low temperature. Food stays fresh for weeks or even months.

Patterns of chemical change

Nice and warm

Look at the pictures about making bread.

Make the dough.

(flour + water + sugar
+ yeast + salt)

Put dough in the tin.

Leave in a warm place.
(25 to 30 °C)

bubbles of carbon dioxide
make the dough rise

Bake in a hot oven.
(230 °C)

Making bread.

5 (a) What makes the dough rise?

(b) Why must the dough be left in a warm place for this to happen?

(c) What happens to the live yeast in the hot oven?

When we make wine we must also keep it at the right temperature.

6 Joe set up three identical fermenting bottles to make strawberry wine. He put one in the kitchen, one in the bedroom and one in the garage.

Five days later he looked at the bottles. The table shows what he saw.

(a) In which bottle was the yeast working most quickly?

(b) Why do you think the yeast in the other two bottles was working more slowly?

(c) Which gas were the bubbles made from?

(d) After 10 days, no more bubbles were made by the bottle in the kitchen. Why not?

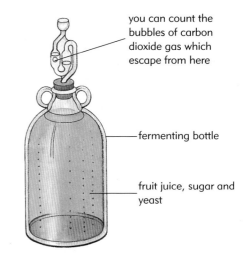

you can count the bubbles of carbon dioxide gas which escape from here

fermenting bottle

fruit juice, sugar and yeast

Making wine.

Where Joe put the fermenting bottles	Number of bubbles per minute on day 5
bedroom (15 °C)	15
kitchen (25 °C)	30
garage (10 °C)	10

What you need to remember [Copy and complete using the **key words**]

Not too hot and not too cold

Food goes bad when _____ _____ feed on it.

We can keep food fresh for longer by keeping it in a _____ or a

_____. This is because living cells use _____ to speed up

their reactions. These work slowly if the temperature is _____.

Useful living cells like yeast work best at temperatures around _____.

Patterns of chemical change

12

What use is nitrogen?

The biggest part of the air is made from a gas called nitrogen. Nitrogen is an unreactive gas. Our bodies don't use the nitrogen in the air, but it is really useful to us in other ways. Chemists can make it into many useful substances.

Name of gas	How much there is in air
nitrogen	78%
oxygen	21%
other gases	1%

1 Look at the table.

(a) How much of the air is nitrogen?

(b) Is this about $\frac{1}{2}$, $\frac{2}{3}$ or $\frac{4}{5}$ of the air?

2 Look at the diagrams.

Write down <u>four</u> things that chemists can make with nitrogen.

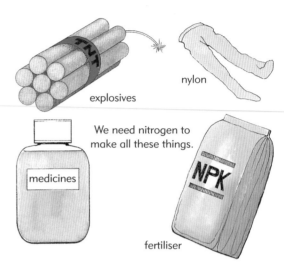

explosives

nylon

medicines

We need nitrogen to make all these things.

NPK

fertiliser

Plants need nitrogen

To grow healthy plants we must give them more than just water. Plants need **nitrogen** to help them grow well.

Plants can't use the nitrogen gas that we find in the air. The nitrogen must be joined with other elements in substances called **nitrates**. These nitrates dissolve in water. Plants can then take them in through their roots.

The pictures show what happens to a plant if it doesn't get enough nitrogen.

3 Copy and complete the following sentences.

Plants need nitrogen to grow healthy _____ and _____. Plants take in nitrogen through their _____ in the form of substances called _____.

4 What does the plant look like that had too little nitrogen?

Plant grown with plenty of nitrogen. Leaves and stem are healthy.

Plant grown with too little nitrogen. Small, yellow leaves and weak stem.

Patterns of chemical change

Why do farmers need fertilisers?

Fertilisers are important to farmers. Plants take nitrates out of the soil when they grow. Farmers often use the same fields year after year. It is important for the farmer to put nitrates back into the soil again.

Chemists can turn the nitrogen from the air into nitrates. This can happen in nature too. Farmers buy nitrates for fertiliser.

5 Look at the fertiliser labels. Write down

(a) <u>one</u> way in which fertilisers A and B are the same

(b) <u>two</u> ways in which the fertilisers are different.

Preparing to spread fertiliser on to fields.

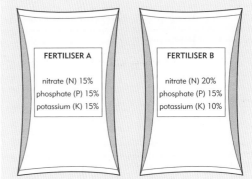

FERTILISER A	FERTILISER B
nitrate (N) 15%	nitrate (N) 20%
phosphate (P) 15%	phosphate (P) 15%
potassium (K) 15%	potassium (K) 10%

Big is best!

Farmers want to grow the best crops possible. The **yield** is the amount of crops that a farmer can grow. Farmers can increase the yield of their crops by using fertilisers.

6 (a) Copy this table. Use the diagram to help you fill it in.

Mass of fertiliser used on field (kg)	Average height of crop (cm)

(b) What happens to the height of the crop as more fertiliser is used? Answer as carefully as you can.

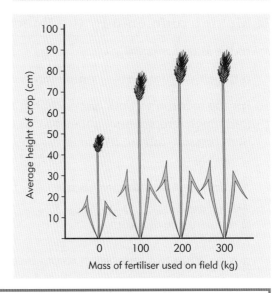

What you need to remember [Copy and complete using the **key words**]

What use is nitrogen?

Plants need _____ for healthy growth.

About _____ of the air is nitrogen but plants can't use nitrogen gas directly.

Instead, the plants take in _____ through their roots.

Farmers add nitrogen to the soil by using _____.

This increases the _____ of their crops.

Patterns of chemical change

13

Catching nitrogen to feed plants

Plants need nitrogen to grow properly but they can't use nitrogen from the air. The nitrogen has to be changed into nitrate.

Chemists make nitrate fertiliser in several steps. In the first step they change nitrogen into a chemical called **ammonia**. They do this using the **Haber process**.

1 (a) Why is the process chemists use to make ammonia called the Haber process?

  (b) How much fertiliser is made each day using this process?

  (c) How much fertiliser is made each year?

> ### REMEMBER
>
> We use a catalyst to speed up a reaction.

This is Fritz Haber. He developed the process for making ammonia from nitrogen and hydrogen. Thanks to him we make over 60 million kilograms of fertiliser containing nitrogen each day.

▨ Making ammonia by the Haber process

In the Haber process

nitrogen + hydrogen ⟶ ammonia

For the reaction to work fast enough it must be at a fairly high temperature (about 400 °C) and at a very high pressure (about 200 times the pressure of the atmosphere).

A catalyst made from iron is used.

2 Look at the diagram.

  (a) What <u>two</u> gases react to produce ammonia?

  (b) Where do these <u>two</u> gases come from?

3 Write down <u>three</u> things that help to produce ammonia faster.

Not all of the nitrogen and hydrogen react.

4 How is the ammonia separated from the unreacted nitrogen and hydrogen?

5 What then happens to the unreacted nitrogen and hydrogen?

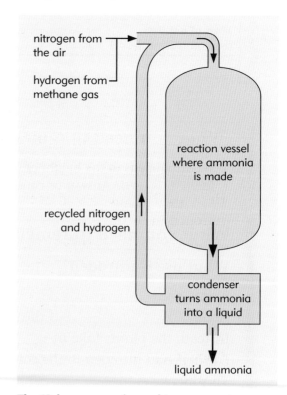

The Haber process for making ammonia.

Patterns of chemical change

Making nitric acid

Some ammonia from the Haber process is then changed into **nitric** acid. The diagram shows how this is done.

6 Copy and complete the following sentences.

When we heat the ammonia with oxygen we make a gas called _____ _____. We react this gas with water and oxygen to make _____ _____.

The first stage of the process is called an **oxidation** reaction.

7 What do we do to make the ammonia and oxygen react more quickly?

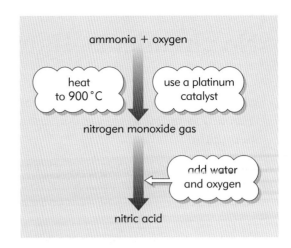

ammonia + oxygen

heat to 900 °C

use a platinum catalyst

nitrogen monoxide gas

add water and oxygen

nitric acid

And finally ...

Farmers can't put corrosive nitric acid on the soil!

8 Why not?

We can change the acid into **ammonium nitrate**. Ammonium nitrate is the most common fertiliser. We make it by adding the nitric acid to more ammonia. We call this reaction **neutralisation**. The ammonia neutralises the nitric acid.

9 Copy and complete the word equation for this reaction.

_____ + _____ ⟶ _____ _____

Ammonium nitrate fertiliser.

What you need to remember

Catching nitrogen to feed plants

Here is a flow chart to show how we can make ammonium nitrate fertiliser from the nitrogen in the air.

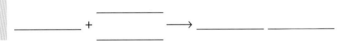

Copy it and fill in the boxes using the **key words**. Some of the boxes have been filled in for you.

Patterns of chemical change

14

No chemicals, thank you

We make fertilisers such as ammonium nitrate in chemical factories. So we say that ammonium nitrate is an <u>artificial</u> fertiliser.

But we can grow healthy plants without using artificial fertilisers. Some people use natural fertilisers to put the nitrogen back into the soil.

Look at the diagrams.

1 Write down <u>three</u> natural ways we can put nitrogen back into the soil.

Natural fertilisers do the same job as artificial fertilisers, because they contain similar chemicals. However, if they just relied on natural fertilisers, farmers wouldn't be able to grow enough food for us all. There just isn't enough natural fertiliser to grow all of the crops that we need.

A compost heap makes fertiliser from rotting waste.

Animal manure is rich in nitrogen and makes a good fertiliser.

Clover has bacteria in its roots. These can change nitrogen from the air into nitrates. Plants can take in these nitrates.

A problem with fertilisers

Many fertilisers contain **nitrates**. Nitrates are good for plants because they contain **nitrogen** that makes plants grow well. But if the nitrates don't stay in the soil then we have a problem. Rain can wash them into our rivers and ponds.

2 Copy and complete the following sentences.

Fertilisers contain _____. If these get into our drinking _____ then they can cause problems.

3 What happens if you swallow nitrates?

4 What happens if nitrates get into rivers and lakes?

If you swallow nitrates, they can get into your blood. Your blood then cannot carry oxygen around your body properly.

Nitrates in lakes and rivers can cause the plants and animals to **die**.

So are fertilisers good or bad?

There are two sides to every argument.

Look at the different things that people say about fertilisers.

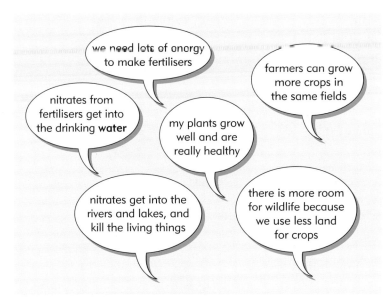

we need lots of energy to make fertilisers

nitrates from fertilisers get into the drinking **water**

my plants grow well and are really healthy

farmers can grow more crops in the same fields

nitrates get into the rivers and lakes, and kill the living things

there is more room for wildlife because we use less land for crops

5 Draw a table like this one and fill it in.

Advantages of using fertilisers	Disadvantages of using fertilisers

6 Imagine that you are an environmental health officer. It is your job to make sure that the environment doesn't harm people's health. You have just read the two newspaper articles. What should you now do?

My best crop ever!

Farmer William Mitchell cannot believe his luck this year. At Mill Farm he has had a bumper wheat harvest in spite of the poor weather.
'I can only think it must be the new fertiliser that I used. These ears of wheat are enormous, they have to be seen to be believed.'

Poisoned water

Three children in Mill St. Newbarton have been admitted to hospital this week. They were all suffering from nitrate poisoning. They were all swimming in the lake by Mill Farm earlier this week.

What you need to remember [Copy and complete using the **key words**]

No chemicals, thank you

Fertilisers contain chemicals called _____. These chemicals give plants the _____ that they need.

Nitrates can cause problems if they get into the _____ supply because they are poisonous.

If nitrates get into rivers and lakes then they can cause all of the living things to

_____.

161

15

How heavy are atoms?

Size of units

We choose units of measurement that make the numbers easy – not too big and not too small.
For example, we measure the length of a piece of paper in centimetres. We measure the length of a room in metres and the length of a journey to the next town in kilometres.

A person.

1 Which units (centimetres, metres or kilometres) would you use to measure the length of

(a) an air journey

(b) a picture frame

(c) a garden?

Sweets.

2 Match up the mass units below with the three things in the drawings. We would use:

(a) grams to measure the mass of _____

(b) kilograms to measure the mass of _____

(c) tonnes to measure the mass of _____

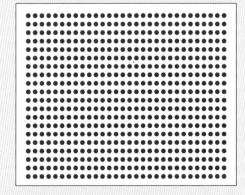

A large ship.

Can we weigh atoms?

Atoms are the very **small** particles that make up all of the elements. Atoms of different elements have different masses.

Atoms are so small that you can't weigh them even with the best scientific balance.

3 Copy and complete the following sentences.

The element made with the heaviest atoms is called

_____.

One atom of this element has a mass of

_____ g.

Numbers as small as this are not easy to write down or use in calculations.

4 Why do we not usually measure the mass of an atom in grams?

Atoms of uranium are the heaviest atoms that we find in nature. Even so there is a huge number of atoms in just 1 gram of uranium. There are lots of dots in this box.

But in 1 gram of uranium, there are over 4 million, million, million times more atoms than dots in the box.

This means that one uranium atom has a mass of 0.0000000000000000000004 g.

Patterns of chemical change

Inventing a scale of mass for weighing atoms

Chemists can't weigh separate atoms. But they can compare how heavy different atoms are.

For example, a carbon atom weighs 12 times as much as a hydrogen atom. So if we say that the lightest atom, **hydrogen**, has a mass of **1 unit**, then a carbon atom has a mass of (12 × 1 units =) 12 units.

We call the mass of an atom in these units its **relative** atomic mass. We use the symbol A_r for short.

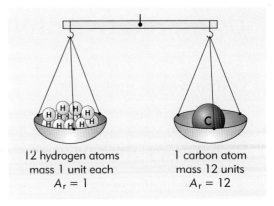

12 hydrogen atoms
mass 1 unit each
$A_r = 1$

1 carbon atom
mass 12 units
$A_r = 12$

5   Copy and complete the following sentence.

   A_r is a quick way of writing _____ _____

   _____.

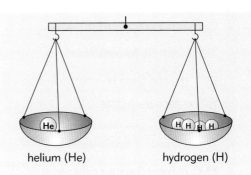

helium (He)   hydrogen (H)

6   Copy and complete the table.

Atom	A_r
hydrogen	
	12
helium	

7   Work out the relative atomic masses of the atoms shown in the diagram below.

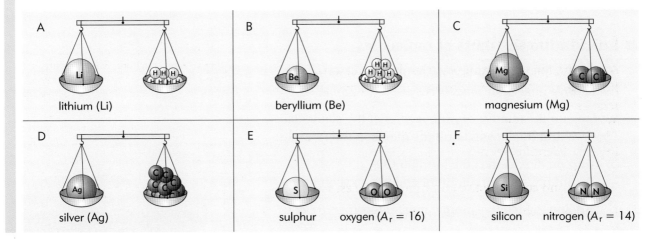

A   lithium (Li)

B   beryllium (Be)

C   magnesium (Mg)

D   silver (Ag)

E   sulphur   oxygen ($A_r = 16$)

F   silicon   nitrogen ($A_r = 14$)

What you need to remember [Copy and complete using the **key words**]

How heavy are atoms?

Atoms are far too _____ to be easily weighed in grams.
We compare the masses of atoms with each other. This is called _____
atomic mass or _____ for short.
The lightest element is _____. It has an A_r of _____ **unit**.

Using relative atomic mass

Can we weigh molecules?

In molecules, atoms are joined together. Substances are called compounds if their molecules are made from atoms of different elements.

1 Copy the picture of the two molecules. Write for each molecule whether it is an element or a compound.

2 Copy and complete the following sentences.

The formula for ammonia is _____.

This means that in one molecule of ammonia there are _____ hydrogen atoms and _____ nitrogen atom.

The formula for nitrogen is _____.

This means that it contains 2 _____ of nitrogen.

We use the relative atomic mass scale to compare the masses of different molecules.

We call the mass of the molecule its relative molecular mass, M_r.

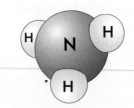

ammonia, formula NH_3

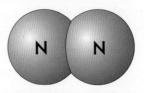

nitrogen, formula N_2

Calculating the mass of molecules

If we know the formula of a molecule then working out the relative molecular mass is easy.

We look up the relative **atomic** masses of the elements. Then we **add** the masses of all the atoms in the formula.

(i) Carbon dioxide has the formula CO_2.
It contains one carbon atom and two oxygen atoms.

Adding the relative atomic masses together, we get:

$$\begin{array}{cccc} C & O & O & CO_2 \end{array}$$
Relative molecular mass = 12 + 16 + 16 = 44

(ii) A molecule of oxygen, formula O_2, has got two oxygen atoms in the molecule. Each oxygen atom has a mass of 16.
Therefore the two oxygen atoms have a total mass of 32.

$$\begin{array}{ccc} O & O & O_2 \end{array}$$
Relative molecular mass = 16 + 16 = 32

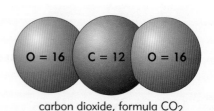

carbon dioxide, formula CO_2

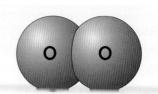

oxygen molecule, formula O_2

3 (a) Draw a molecule of ammonia.

(b) Write the relative atomic mass of each atom on your diagram.

(c) Now work out the relative molecular mass (M_r) for ammonia.

4 Calculate the relative molecular mass, M_r, for nitrogen in the same way.

■ Calculating more relative molecular masses

Here are some rules for reading a chemical formula.

Each element has a chemical symbol (e.g. H = hydrogen, O = oxygen).

A chemical symbol without a number stands for one atom of that element. So in H_2O (water) there is one atom of oxygen.

The little number to the right of a symbol tells you how many atoms there are of that element only. So, in water there are two hydrogen atoms.

5 The formula for copper sulphate is $CuSO_4$. It has four atoms of oxygen but only one atom each of copper and sulphur.

(a) How many atoms of copper does it have?

(b) How many atoms of sulphur does it have?

(c) How many atoms of oxygen does it have?

The number to the right of a bracket gives us the number of atoms of every element inside the bracket.

So, in $Ca(OH)_2$ there are two atoms of oxygen and two atoms of hydrogen.

6 Now calculate the relative molecular mass for each compound shown in the diagram.

The relative atomic masses of some elements.

Element	Symbol	A_r
aluminium	Al	27
bromine	Br	80
calcium	Ca	40
carbon	C	12
chlorine	Cl	35.5
copper	Cu	64
helium	He	4
hydrogen	H	1
iron	Fe	56
krypton	Kr	84
magnesium	Mg	24
nitrogen	N	14
oxygen	O	16
sulphur	S	32

You need some of these to do question 6.

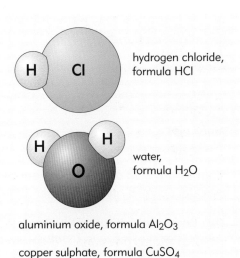

hydrogen chloride, formula HCl

water, formula H_2O

aluminium oxide, formula Al_2O_3

copper sulphate, formula $CuSO_4$

calcium hydroxide, formula $Ca(OH)_2$

What you need to remember [Copy and complete using the **key words**]

Using relative atomic mass

To work out a relative molecular mass (_____ for short):

■ look up the relative _____ masses of the elements,

■ then _____ together the masses of all the atoms in the formula.

Elementary pie

Think about an apple pie you buy from the supermarket. There is usually a table of information on the packet. This tells us how much carbohydrate, fat and protein there is in each 100 g of the pie.

1 Write down how much of each type of food substance there is in 100 g of the pie. Write the list in order starting with what there is most of.

Telling you how much of everything there is in each 100 g makes it easy to compare different foods.

2 How do the amounts of protein and fat in the apple pie compare with the amounts in the bread?

Another way of saying 8g out of 100g is to say 8 per cent. Per cent means 'out of one hundred'.

Apple pie Nutritional information Average values per 100 g	
protein	3 g
carbohydrate	54 g
fat	11 g

Bread Nutritional information Average values per 100 g	
protein	8 g
carbohydrate	31 g
fat	2 g

How much of an element is in a compound?

We can easily see how many units of mass of **elements** are in a compound.

For example, sulphur dioxide is SO_2.

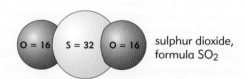

sulphur dioxide, formula SO_2

$$
\begin{array}{llll}
M_r & = \text{mass of S atom} + \text{mass of 2 O atoms} \\
\text{(relative} & = & 32 & + & 2 \times 16 \\
\text{molecular} & = & 32 & + & 32 \\
\text{mass)} & = & & 64
\end{array}
$$

Sulphur gives 32 units of mass out of 64 for sulphur dioxide. Oxygen gives the other 32 units of mass.

This means that sulphur dioxide is 50 per cent sulphur and 50 per cent oxygen by mass.

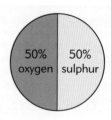

Half is the same as 50%.

3 Now work out the percentage by mass of carbon and hydrogen in methane one step at at time, like this:

(a) What is the mass of all the hydrogen atoms?

(b) What is the mass of the carbon atom?

(c) What is the relative molecular mass of methane?

(d) What is the percentage by mass of hydrogen in methane?

(e) What is the percentage by mass of carbon in methane?

methane, formula CH_4

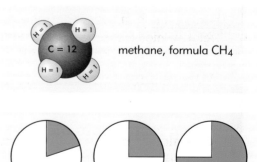

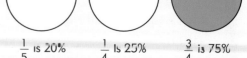

$\frac{1}{5}$ is 20% $\frac{1}{4}$ is 25% $\frac{3}{4}$ is 75%

How to calculate percentages

Percentages don't usually work out as easily as they do for sulphur dioxide and methane.

In water, for example, 2 parts out of 18 are hydrogen.

To calculate this as a %

    press the number 2
    then press ÷
    then press the numbers 1 then 8 (18)
    then press %

4 What is 2 out of 18 as a percentage?

You can work out other awkward percentages in a similar way.

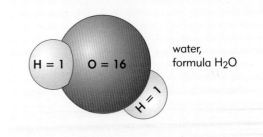

water, formula H_2O

The percentages by mass of elements in ammonia

The diagram shows an ammonia molecule.

5 Work out:

    (a) the total mass of hydrogen atoms in the molecule

    (b) the relative molecular mass, M_r, for the molecule

    (c) the percentage by mass of hydrogen in the molecule.

6 Work out the percentage by mass of nitrogen in ammonia. (Hint: what percentage isn't hydrogen?)

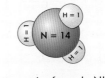

ammonia, formula NH_3

> General percentage rule
>
> The percentage by mass of an element in a compound
>
> $$= \frac{\text{total mass of the element}}{\text{relative molecular mass of the compound}} \times 100$$

What you need to remember [Copy and complete using the **key words**]

Elementary pie

Chemical compounds are made of _____ (just as an apple pie is made of ingredients).

[You need to be able to work out the percentage by mass of each element in a compound, just like you have on these pages.]

18 Drawing diagrams of chemical apparatus

When we do an experiment, we often need to draw a diagram. Adding a diagram to our written notes makes it easier to show what happened in the experiment.

Drawing diagrams of containers

The simplest container we can use is a **test tube**. We can heat solids or liquids in a test tube.
For bigger volumes of liquid we use a **beaker** or a **flask**. We can use round flasks or conical flasks.
We can use an **evaporating basin** to grow crystals from a solution.

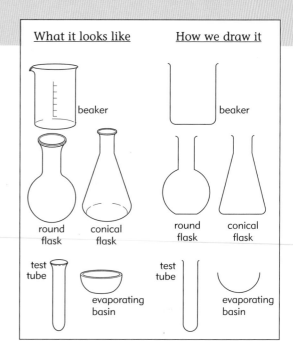

What it looks like	How we draw it
beaker	beaker
round flask	conical flask	round flask	conical flask
test tube	evaporating basin	test tube	evaporating basin

Measuring the liquids we need

Most beakers have a scale marked on the outside. This gives a rough idea of the volume of liquid inside. We can use a **measuring cylinder** if we need to measure liquids more carefully.
A **burette** lets us measure liquids very accurately.

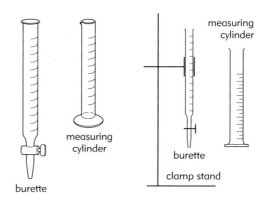

measuring cylinder

burette

measuring cylinder

burette

clamp stand

Special apparatus that we use with gases

We can collect many kinds of gas in a **gas jar**. If we want to measure an amount of gas, we can use a **gas syringe** which has a scale on it.

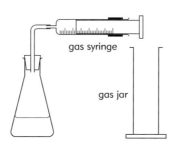

gas syringe

gas jar

Filtering mixtures to separate them

We need a **filter funnel** and some **filter paper** to separate sand from a solution. The solution goes through the filter paper but the sand does not. The job of the filter funnel is to support the filter paper.

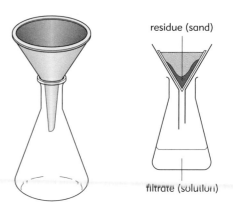

residue (sand)

filtrate (solution)

Patterns of chemical change

▓ Making things hotter

Many experiments need a **Bunsen burner** to make them work. We can use the gas burner to heat test tubes or to set things on fire, such as magnesium ribbon. We also need a **tripod** and a metal **gauze** to hold beakers or flasks.

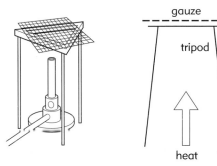

▓ Distilling liquids

We need a **condenser** to turn steam back into water. It also works with other liquids such as alcohol.

This is how we draw the distilling apparatus.

▓ An experiment shown in diagrams

Look at the diagrams below for the experiment to separate a mixture of water, sand, salt and iron filings.

1 Write down the names of the <u>six</u> pieces of apparatus that have a mark like this *.

2 Draw a diagram, using the six pieces of apparatus from question 1, to show how you could produce salt and water from a salt solution that also contained sand.

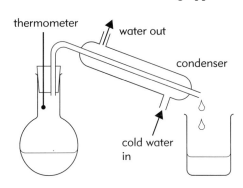

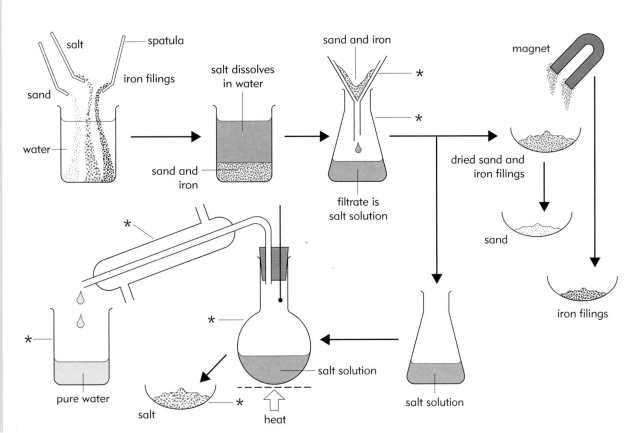

Patterns of chemical change

Knowing when to be careful

We have to be careful when we use some substances. This is because the substances may harm us in some way. When we use harmful substances, we need to look for warnings on the labels. The labels usually have **hazard symbols**. There are different hazard symbols for substances that harm us in different ways.

Starting a fire
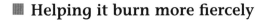

Some substances catch fire very easily. We call these **highly flammable** substances.

1 The label on a bottle of methylated spirits says:

Keep container tightly closed. No smoking.

Why does the label say this?

highly flammable

This symbol appears on labels for substances like methylated spirits.

Helping it burn more fiercely

When things burn they use up oxygen from the air. Some substances contain oxygen, which lets other materials burn even better. We say that substances like this are **oxidising** substances.

2 Sodium chlorate is a strong weedkiller. It can kill all the weeds on a garden path.

A gardener may store sodium chlorate in a garden shed near dry sacks and wood. Why is this a bad idea?

oxidising

This symbol appears on labels for substances like sodium chlorate.

Don't take chances with these materials

Pirate flags used to have a skull and crossbones. Pirates were dangerous and could kill you! Substances that can kill you are called **toxic** substances.

We use <u>tiny</u> amounts of chlorine to kill dangerous bacteria in our drinking water. We also use chlorine to treat the water in swimming pools. But if you breathe in a <u>lot</u> of chlorine it can kill you.

3 Why do we add a little chlorine to the water in a swimming pool?

toxic

This symbol appears on labels for substances like chlorine.

Still bad, but at least it won't kill you

Some substances are **harmful**, but they are not as dangerous as toxic materials.

Copper sulphate forms beautiful blue crystals, but if you swallow solid copper sulphate or some of its solution, it is harmful.

4 A student used copper sulphate to grow crystals. Why should she wash her hands before eating food?

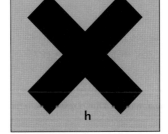
harmful

This symbol appears on labels for substances like copper sulphate.

There is more than one way to get burned

If you touch the inside of a hot oven you will burn yourself. There are chemicals that can destroy your skin and damage your eyes. We call these **corrosive** materials. Corrosive materials can give skin burns.

5 Sulphuric acid is used in experiments and to fill up car batteries. Why should you use safety glasses when using sulphuric acid?

corrosive

This symbol appears on labels for substances like sulphuric acid.

Some substances are irritants

Some substances can make your skin go red or form blisters. If the substance is a dry powder it may make you cough. We call substances like this **irritants**. They are less dangerous than corrosive materials but you must still take care.

Copper carbonate is a beautiful green colour. We can use copper carbonate to make copper metal. If you spill the green powder and breathe it in, it can make you cough. We call the powder an irritant.

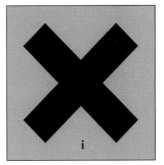
irritant

This symbol appears on labels for substances like copper carbonate.

What you need to remember [Copy and complete using the **key words**]

Knowing when to be careful

Some substances have warning signs on them called _____ _____.

If a material catches fire easily it is _____ _____.

If a material helps other substances to burn by supplying oxygen, we say it is an _____ substance.

We say that substances that can kill you are _____. Less dangerous substances are called _____.

The skin can be destroyed or burned by _____ substances.

Substances that can redden your skin or make you cough are _____.

Handling data

In tests and examinations, you will be asked to interpret scientific data. This data may be presented in several different ways.

▥ Pie charts

The gases in air

The pie charts show how much there is of the main gases in air.

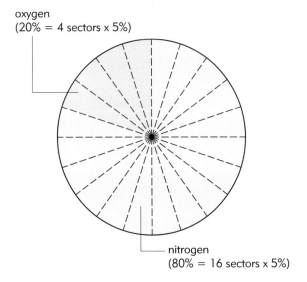

oxygen
(20% = 4 sectors x 5%)

nitrogen
(80% = 16 sectors x 5%)

Approximate figures.

You may be asked to <u>compare</u> the amounts of nitrogen and oxygen in the air.

You could say that there is <u>more</u> nitrogen than oxygen.

A better answer is to say that there is (about) <u>four times as much</u> nitrogen as oxygen.

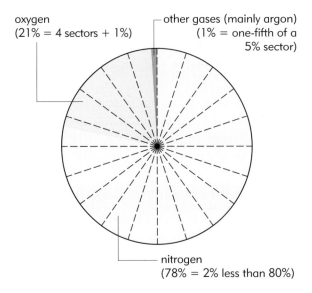

oxygen
(21% = 4 sectors + 1%)

other gases (mainly argon)
(1% = one-fifth of a 5% sector)

nitrogen
(78% = 2% less than 80%)

More accurate figures.

You may be asked to complete a pie chart.

Remember:

■ to draw thin, straight lines through the centre of the circle

■ to mark off each 1% in some of the sectors if you need to, like this

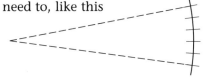

■ to add labels, or use a key like this

nitrogen	
oxygen	
other gases	

▦ Bar charts

Comparing the strengths of metals

The bar chart shows the force you need to break wires of different metals by stretching them. The wires are all the same thickness.

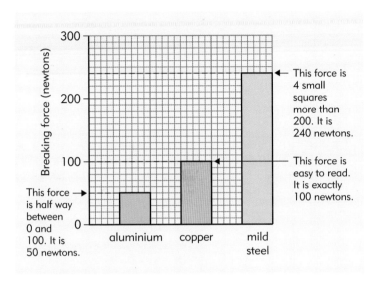

You may be asked to put the figures into a table like this:

Metal	Breaking force in N
aluminium	50
copper	100
mild steel	240

You may be asked to draw bars on a bar chart.

Remember:

- to look carefully at the scale

- to draw the bars the same thickness and equally spaced out

- to draw the top of each bar with a thin, straight line

- to label each bar or colour the bars and draw a key like this

aluminium	
copper	
mild steel	

▦ Sankey diagrams

Where does the candle wax go?

The diagram shows what happens to each 100 g of wax when a candle burns.

Remember, all the candle wax must go somewhere:

$$80 g + 15 g + 5 g = 100 g$$

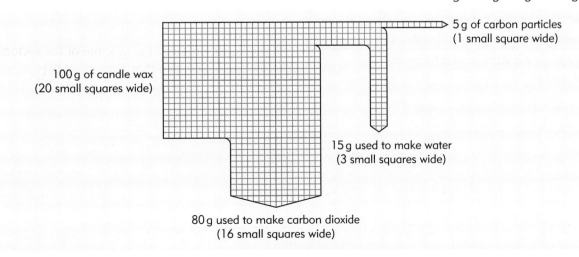

Line graphs

Watching a chemical reaction

You can make hydrogen gas by dropping some magnesium ribbon into dilute acid. The graph shows how fast the hydrogen is produced.

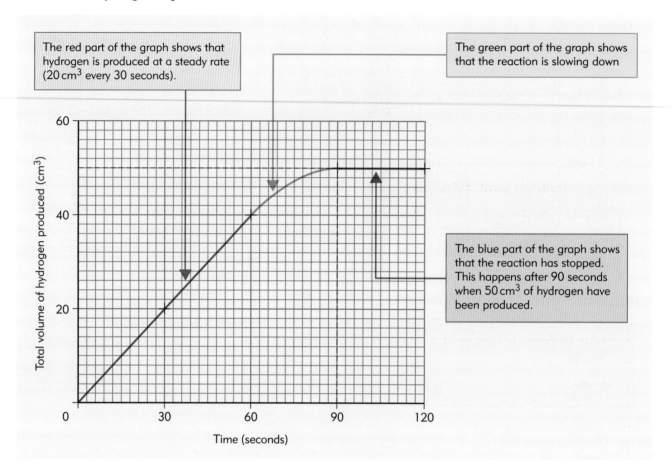

The red part of the graph shows that hydrogen is produced at a steady rate (20 cm^3 every 30 seconds).

The green part of the graph shows that the reaction is slowing down

The blue part of the graph shows that the reaction has stopped. This happens after 90 seconds when 50 cm^3 of hydrogen have been produced.

You may be asked to plot a line graph from a table of results like this:

Volume of hydrogen in cm^3	0	20	40	50	50
Time in seconds	start	30	60	90	120

Remember

- to look carefully at the scales

- to label both of the axes

- to mark the points carefully like this ⊞ or ⊡

- to draw a line through the points using a sharp pencil

  – draw any straight parts of the graph using a ruler

  – draw any curved parts of the graph without bumps

Revising for tests and examinations

Stage 1

See if you know which words go into the **What you need to remember** boxes for the pages you are revising.

Try to do this <u>without</u> looking at the text or diagrams on the pages.

Then, if there is anything that you can't do, read the text and look at the diagrams to find the answer.

Remember

■ the key words are printed like this

reactivity   water   displaces   pop

■ you can check your answers at the back of the book (pages 176–186).

But you don't just have to <u>remember</u> the scientific ideas.

You also need to be able to <u>use</u> these ideas.

You may be asked to do this in a situation you haven't met before.

Example
Most metals corrode in damp air.

If you join two metals together:

■ the more reactive metal corrodes even faster

■ the less reactive metal doesn't corrode until all the other metal has corroded.

(a) Why are magnesium blocks attached to the iron pipes that carry North Sea gas?

(b) Why should you not use copper washers with iron bolts?

Answers
(a) The magnesium corrodes more quickly. This stops the iron pipe corroding.

(b) Using copper washers would make the iron bolts corrode more quickly.

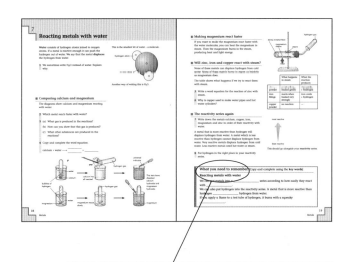

What you need to remember [Copy and complete using the **key words**]

Reacting metals with water

We can put metals into a ___reactivity___ series according to how easily they react with ___water___.

We can also put hydrogen into the reactivity series. A metal that is more reactive than hydrogen ___displaces___ hydrogen from water.

If you apply a flame to a test tube of hydrogen, it burns with a squeaky ___pop___.

Stage 2

See if you can <u>use</u> the ideas you have revised.

There are lots of questions in the text which ask you to do this.

Your teacher should be able to give you some extra questions.

Some of these may have been used in examinations in previous years.

Metals

1 What's special about metals

All metals, except mercury, are **solids** at room temperature. Metals usually have **high** melting points. Newly cut metal surfaces are **shiny**.
Metals are good conductors of both **heat** and **electricity**.
Metals like steel can carry large weights. We say they are **strong**.
When you hammer metals:
■ they don't usually break; we say that they are **tough**
■ they may change their **shape**.

2 Making the most of metals (1)

We use metals when they have the right **properties** for the job we want them to do. For example, copper is used in electrical **cables** because it is a good **conductor** of electricity.
We can change the properties of a metal by mixing it with other metals. This mixture is called an **alloy**.
Mixing copper with zinc or tin makes alloys that are **harder** than copper.

3 Making the most of metals (2)

Aluminium is a very **lightweight** metal.
It is also quite a good **conductor** of electricity.
Aluminium doesn't corrode because of a tough, thin layer of **aluminium oxide**. Aluminium can be mixed with magnesium. This makes an alloy that is **harder** and **stronger** than aluminium.
Steel is a tough, strong, cheap and easily shaped metal. To stop it rusting we can alloy it with **nickel** and **chromium**. This is called **stainless** steel.

4 How many metals are there?

About three-quarters of the elements are **metals**.
You can mix these to make metals called **alloys**.

5 What's special about non-metals?

About one-**quarter** of the elements are non-metals.
Most non-metals have **low** melting points.
Half of the non-metals are **gases**.
The rest are solids apart from **bromine**, which is a liquid.
Solid non-metals usually look **dull**. They usually break or crumble when we hit them; we say they are **brittle**.
They are usually **poor** conductors of heat and electricity.

6 Burning metals

Most metals react with **oxygen**.
Some metals react more easily than others; we say that they are more **reactive**. We can list metals in order of their reactivity. This is called a reactivity **series**.

7 Reacting metals with water

We can put metals into a **reactivity** series according to how easily they react with **water**.
We can also put hydrogen into the reactivity series. A metal that is more reactive than hydrogen **displaces** hydrogen from water.
If you apply a flame to a test tube of hydrogen, it burns with a squeaky **pop**.

8 Reacting metals with acids

Some metals react with dilute acids; **hydrogen** gas is produced. This reaction happens with metals that are more **reactive** than hydrogen.

9 Competing metals

A more reactive metal will push a **less** reactive metal out of its compounds. We say that it **displaces** the less reactive metal.
We can also put carbon into the **reactivity** series because it can displace a less reactive **metal** from a metal oxide.

10 Where do metals come from?

Metals are found in the Earth's **crust**.
Most metals, except gold, are found joined with other **elements** as compounds.
Compounds of metals and oxygen are called **oxides**.
Rocks containing metal compounds are called **ores**.
Copper and iron are extracted from their oxides by heating them with **carbon**.
Removing the oxygen from a metal oxide is called **reduction**.
Aluminium oxide can only be reduced using **electricity**.

11 How do we get all the steel we use?

Iron is extracted from iron ore in a **blast** furnace.
The high temperature needed is produced by burning **coke** in the hot **air** that is blasted into the furnace.
This makes carbon **dioxide** gas.
The carbon dioxide then reacts with more carbon to make carbon **monoxide** gas.
Carbon is more **reactive** than iron, so carbon monoxide takes the oxygen from iron oxide. This gives the metal iron and a gas called carbon **dioxide**.
The carbon monoxide **reduces** the iron oxide to iron metal.
Solid waste materials in the iron ore react with **limestone** to make **slag**.
The furnace is so hot that the iron and slag both **melt** and run down to the base of the furnace.

12 Using electricity to split up metal compounds

Electrically charged atoms are called **ions**.
You can split up a metal compound by passing **electricity** through it.
You can do this only if you **melt** the compound by heating it, or **dissolve** the compound in water.
This means that the ions in the compound can **move** about.
Using electricity to split up a compound is called **electrolysis**. We say that the compound has been **decomposed**.
The metal ions in a compound have a **positive** charge.
During electrolysis, the metal ions move towards the **negative** electrode.

13 How do we get all the aluminium we need?

We can extract aluminium from the compound aluminium **oxide**. Aluminium oxide melts at a very **high** temperature.
We can lower the melting temperature by adding a substance called **cryolite**.
The electrodes are made of **carbon**.
Since the temperature is high and oxygen is given off, the **positive** electrode burns away.
Molten **aluminium** collects at the base.

16 The bad taste guide to acids and alkalis

We must handle acids with care because they are **corrosive**.
This is especially true when they are strong.
Acids **dissolve** in water to make colourless solutions.
The opposites of acids are **alkalis**. These substances are also corrosive.
Alkalis also dissolve in water to give **colourless** solutions.
Water is neither an acid nor an alkali. It is **neutral**.
Many **aqueous** or watery solutions are neutral.

17 Colour me red when acidic

To show whether solutions are acidic, alkaline or neutral, we use **indicators**.
Indicators are dyes that change **colour** in acids or alkalis.
We measure the strength of an acid or alkali by its **pH** number.

The pH scale

0 1 2 3 4 5 6 7 8 9 10 11 12 13 14

increasingly **acidic** ⬅ ⬆ ➡ increasingly **alkaline**
At pH 7, a solution is **neutral**.

18 Acids and alkalis can cancel each other out

When we add an acid to an alkali they **neutralise** each other.
This reaction is called **neutralisation**.
An acid will neutralise an **alkali**.
An alkali will neutralise an **acid**.
We can check whether neutralisation has taken place by using an **indicator**.

19 Neutralisation – where do the acid and alkali go?

Acid + alkali ⟶ **salt + water**

To make:

- a sodium salt you use **sodium** hydroxide with an acid
- a potassium salt you use **potassium** hydroxide with an acid
- a chloride you use **hydrochloric** acid with an alkali
- a nitrate you use **nitric** acid with an alkali
- a sulphate you use **sulphuric** acid with an alkali

20 Making some acids and alkalis from elements

Non-metals such as sulphur, carbon and nitrogen react with oxygen to produce compounds called **oxides**.

These dissolve in water to make **acidic** solutions.

If metal hydroxides dissolve in water, they make **alkaline** solutions.

Metals which have hydroxides that dissolve in water include **sodium** and **potassium**.

Calcium hydroxide only partly dissolves in water.

Earth materials

1 Limestone – a useful rock

Limestone is a common **rock**. We get limestone from **quarries**.

Limestone is very useful for **buildings** because it is easy to cut into blocks.

The chemical in limestone is **calcium carbonate**.

When we heat limestone strongly in a kiln it turns into **quicklime**.

The chemical name for quicklime is **calcium oxide**.

2 What can we do with quicklime?

Quicklime **reacts** strongly with cold water. It forms a new material called **slaked lime**.

This has the chemical name of **calcium hydroxide**.

Slaked lime is an **alkali**, it can neutralise acids.

Most plants do not grow well in acidic soils.

Farmers use slaked lime to make soils less **acidic**.

3 Other useful materials made from limestone

We heat limestone and clay together in a hot kiln to make **cement**. A mixture of cement, sand, rock and water gives **concrete**.

The water **reacts** with the cement and makes the concrete set solid.

Glass is a very useful material. You need to heat a mixture of limestone, sand and **soda** to make glass. Soda has the chemical name **sodium carbonate**.

We can melt old glass and use it again. We say that the glass has been **recycled**.

4 Rocks made from hot liquid

The Earth has a **crust** of solid rock on the outside.

Under this is hot, molten rock called **magma**.

Rocks that form when hot, molten rock cools down are called **igneous** rocks. Magma that flows outside the crust is called **lava**. Basalt forms from lava that has cooled outside the crust, so we say it is an **extrusive** igneous rock. Basalt cools quickly, so it contains **small** crystals.

Granite forms from magma that has cooled inside the crust. We say it is an **intrusive** igneous rock. Granite cools slowly, so it contains **large** crystals.

5 Rocks made from bits of other rocks

Layers of **sand** and mud pile up at the bottom of lakes and seas. These are called **sediment**.

Over millions of years, the weight of the sediment squeezes out the water. Natural chemicals then stick the bits together, and we say that the bits have been **cemented**. The rock that is formed is a kind of **sedimentary** rock.

Sandstone is a sedimentary rock made from bits of sand. Limestone contains bits of **shells**. This is why limestone is mainly made of the chemical **calcium carbonate**.

6 Which are the oldest rocks?

With sedimentary rocks:
> the layer at the bottom is usually the **oldest**,
> the layer at the top is usually the **youngest**.

This is usually true even when the rocks have been moved, for example **tilted**, **faulted** or **folded**.

It is not true if the rocks have been turned **upside down**.

Sedimentary rocks often contain the remains of **plants** and **animals** that lived at the time the sediment was laid down.

We call these remains **fossils**.

Rocks with the same fossils are probably the same **age**.

7 Rocks that have changed

Deep inside the Earth's crust there can be high **pressure** and high **temperature**. These can change rocks.

We call the changed rocks **metamorphic** rocks.

Limestone can be changed into **marble**, and mudstone can be changed into **slate**.

The changed rocks look different, they have a different **structure**. The changed rocks also feel different, they have a different **texture**.

Some metamorphic rocks have bands of **crystals**.

9 The Earth

The Earth is shaped like a ball. We say it is nearly **spherical**.

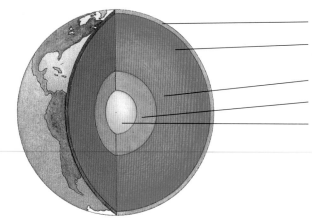

(i) The **crust** is made of solid rock.

(ii) The outer **mantle** is made of **magma**. This is thick and sticky molten rock. We say it is very **viscous**.

(iii) The inner mantle is made of solid rock.

(iv) The **outer** core is made of liquid iron and nickel.

(v) The inner **core** is made of solid **iron** and **nickel**. These metals make the Earth much **denser**.

10 Movements that make mountains

The Earth's crust is cracked into large pieces. We call these **tectonic plates**. The plates **move** very slowly, just a few **centimetres** each year.

Millions of years ago, South America and Africa were next to each other. We know this because:

■ their **shapes** fit together well

■ they have rocks containing the same **fossils**.

In some places, tectonic plates push together. This forces some rocks upwards and makes new **mountains**.

11 What keeps the Earth's crust moving?

Tectonic plates move because of **convection** currents in the **magma** below the Earth's crust.

The energy that produces the currents comes from **radioactive** substances inside the Earth.

13 Where does oil come from?

We find oil in the Earth's **crust**. This is called **crude oil**.

Oil was made from things that lived in the sea **millions** of years ago.

Fuels that are made from dead plants or animals are called **fossil** fuels.

Two other fossil fuels are **coal** and **natural gas**.

Oil **floats** on water so it rises up through **permeable** rocks.

When the oil reaches an impermeable rock it becomes **trapped**.

To get this oil we need to **drill** down through the layers of impermeable rock.

14 Oil – what would we do without it?

Crude oil is a **mixture** of many different substances. Some parts of the oil can be burned as **fuels**.
We can also use the chemicals in oil to make new **materials**.

15 How crude oil is split up into parts

When you heat a liquid it **evaporates** to form a vapour.

When you cool a vapour it **condenses** to form a liquid.

Evaporating a liquid and then condensing it again is called **distillation**.

Separating a mixture of liquids like this is called **fractional distillation**.

The liquids in the mixture must have different **boiling points**.

Crude oil is separated into fractions in **fractionating towers**.

16 What are the chemicals in crude oil?

Substances that contain more than one kind of atom are called **compounds**.

Most of the compounds in crude oil are made from two kinds of atoms. These are **hydrogen** atoms and **carbon** atoms. We call these compounds **hydrocarbons**.

The smallest part of each hydrocarbon is called a **molecule**.

Hydrocarbons with the highest boiling points have the **largest** molecules.

17 Different hydrocarbons for different jobs

Small hydrocarbon molecules can:
    evaporate quickly (we say they are very **volatile**)
    catch fire easily (we say they are very **flammable**)
    pour easily (we say they are not very **viscous**)
Larger hydrocarbons do not have these **properties** and so they are not very good **fuels**.
Large hydrocarbon molecules can be split up into smaller molecules that are more useful. We call this **cracking**.

18 Plastics from oil

Plastics have very **long** molecules. To make plastics we need to **join** together lots of small molecules.
The word 'poly' means 'many', so we say that plastics are **polymers**.
Two common plastics are **polythene** and **PVC**.

19 Burning fuels – where do they go?

When fuels burn they react with **oxygen** from the air.
The new substances that are produced are mainly **gases** that escape into the air.
The atoms in fuels join up with oxygen atoms to form compounds called **oxides**.
When hydrocarbons burn:
■ hydrogen atoms join up with oxygen atoms to make **water** molecules
■ carbon atoms join up with oxygen atoms to make **carbon dioxide** molecules.
Another word for burning is **combustion**.

20 Dangers with fuels

When hydrocarbons burn completely, the carbon atoms join up with oxygen atoms to make **carbon dioxide**.
If there isn't enough oxygen you can get:
■ lots of tiny bits of **carbon**
■ a poisonous gas called **carbon monoxide**.

21 It's raining acid

Acid rain can harm buildings and living things.
When we burn fuels that contain sulphur we make the gas called **sulphur dioxide**.
This gas dissolves in water droplets to make **sulphuric** acid.
The heat from burning fuels makes oxygen and **nitrogen** from the air react together. This makes gases called **nitrogen oxides**.
These gases dissolve in water to produce **nitric** acid.

22 How are we changing the air around us?

The air around us has been almost the **same** for millions of years.
Nearly $\frac{4}{5}$ of the air is **nitrogen** and just over $\frac{1}{5}$ is **oxygen**.
When we burn fuels we make large amounts of **carbon dioxide** gas.
Too much carbon dioxide in the air could make the temperature of the Earth rise.
We call this **global warming**.
We say that carbon dioxide is a **greenhouse** gas.

Structure and bonding

1 Two kinds of stuff

One of the ways scientists sort materials is into **solids** and **liquids**.

Solids stay the same **shape** and always have the same volume.

We can pour liquids into different containers. The liquid takes the shape of the container but it still has the same **volume**.

When a solid turns into a liquid we say that it **melts**. The temperature at which it does this is called its **melting point**.

When a liquid turns into a solid we say that it **freezes**.

2 Stuff you hardly know is there

You can squeeze a **gas** into a smaller space; you can **compress** it. A gas **spreads** out to fill all the space it can.

When a liquid changes to a gas we call it **evaporating**.

When a gas turns into a liquid we call it **condensing**.

Solids, liquids and gases are the three **states** of matter.

3 Making up a model

Scientists believe that everything is made up of tiny **particles**.

Solids and liquids take up the same amount of space because their particles are **close** together.

Particles in solids can only **vibrate** (move about from side to side), so the solid stays the same **shape**.

You can pour a liquid because the particles **move** over each other.

Some solids seem to disappear if we put them in a liquid.

We say that the solid **dissolves** in the liquid. The solid particles separate and spread out through the **particles** of the liquid.

4 A particle model of gases

We can weigh gases but they are very **light** compared to solids or liquids.

This is because the particles in a gas are a long way apart.

We can squash or **compress** gases more than solids or liquids.

This is also because the gas particles are so spread out.

5 Why gases get everywhere

Gases spread out to fill all the **space** they can. This is because gas particles **move** about very fast. We call the spreading out of gases **diffusion**.

6 How substances can change their state

If we heat up a solid the particles gain more **energy**. The particles then start to break away from each other; the solid is now **melting**.

The particles in a liquid can escape if they get enough energy. When this happens we say the liquid **evaporates**.

If we heat up a liquid the particles can escape more **quickly**.

Large bubbles of gas form in a liquid when we make the liquid **boil**.

7 Elements and compounds

All substances are made from tiny **atoms**.

If the substance has atoms that are all of one type, we call it an **element**.

Substances made from atoms of different elements joined together are called **compounds**.

We use letters to stand for elements. We call these **symbols**.

The **formula** of a compound tells us which atoms are in the compound.

8 How to describe chemical reactions

We can describe a chemical reaction using a **word equation**.

The substances that react are the **reactants**.

The new substances that are produced are the **products**.

We can replace the names of each reactant and product by writing its **formula**. The equation for the reaction is now called a **symbol equation**.

In a symbol equation, (s) stands for **solid**, (l) stands for **liquid**, **(g)** stands for gas, **(aq)** stands for aqueous solution.

9 The alkali metals – a chemical family

The elements in Group 1 are called the **alkali metals**. We need to keep them under oil because they are very **reactive**.
Alkali metals react with water to produce **hydrogen gas**.
A solution of the alkali metal **hydroxide** is also produced.
An indicator shows that the solution is **alkaline**.
Alkali metals react with some **non-metals**, such as oxygen. For example:

> sodium + oxygen $\longrightarrow$ **sodium oxide**

10 The halogens – another chemical family

The elements that are 'salt makers' are called **halogens**.
These elements are all in **Group 7** of the Periodic Table.
Atoms of the halogens join up in pairs. We call these pairs **molecules**.
Halogens react with metals to form compounds we call **halides**. These compounds are part of a family of compounds called **salts**.
Halogens also react with other **non-metals** such as hydrogen and carbon.

11 What are atoms made of?

The centre of an atom is called the **nucleus**. This can contain two kinds of particle:
- particles with a positive charge called **protons**
- particles with no charge called **neutrons**.

Atoms of the same element always have the same number of protons. So every element has its own special **proton** number.
The total number of protons and neutrons is called the **mass** number.
Atoms of the same element that have different numbers of neutrons are called **isotopes**.
Around the nucleus there are particles with a negative charge called **electrons**.

12 Making a map of the chemical elements

Helium, neon and argon belong to the family of **noble gases**.
These gases are chemically **unreactive**.
In the **Periodic Table** the elements are arranged:
- in order of how many **protons** they have in their atoms
- so that elements in the same family are in the same column, called a **Group**.

The noble gases are in **Group 0** of the Periodic Table.

13 The Periodic Table of all the elements

In the middle of the Periodic Table there is a block of elements we call the **transition** metals.
These metals usually have **high** melting points.
They are often used as **catalysts** to speed up chemical reactions.
The **compounds** of transition metals often have bright colours.
Two commonly used transition metals are **iron** and **copper**.

15 Differences between elements in the same Group

The further down Group 1 you go:
- the lower the **melting points** and the **boiling points** are, and
- the more **reactive** the metals are.

The further **down** Group 7 you go:
- the higher the melting points and boiling points are, and
- the halogens become less **reactive**.

A more reactive halogen **displaces** a less reactive halogen from its compounds.

16 Why are there families of elements?

In atoms the electrons are arranged in certain **energy levels**. The first level has the **lowest** energy. The lowest level can take up to **two** electrons. The second and third energy levels can each take up to **eight** electrons. Elements in the same Group have the same number of electrons in their **top** energy level.

17 Why elements react to form compounds

When a metal reacts with a non-metal, the metal atoms always give away **electrons**. They form ions that have a **positive** charge.
The non-metal atoms take electrons. They form **ions** that have a **negative** charge.
The substances produced are called **ionic substances**.

18 How atoms of non-metals can join together

Atoms of non-metal elements can join by **sharing** electrons.

When atoms join together in this way they form a **molecule**.

Substances made of molecules are called **molecular** substances.

19 Some differences between ionic and molecular substances

Molecular substances have **low** melting points and boiling points.

This is because there are only weak forces **between** molecules. There are strong bonds between the atoms inside each **molecule**.

Ionic substances form **giant** structures of ions. This is why they have **high** melting points and boiling points.

Carbon atoms in diamond form a giant structure by **sharing** electrons.

We should be able to work out the formula of an ionic substance if we are told the charges on each ion. This is because the electrical charges in an ionic substance must **balance**.

20 Salt – a very useful substance

The chemical name for salt is **sodium chloride**.

It contains the alkali metal **sodium** and the halogen **chlorine**.

We find salt dissolved in the **sea** and buried **underground**.

A solution of salt in water is called **brine**.

Electrolysis of brine produces useful new substances.

At the positive electrode we get **chlorine**, which **bleaches** damp indicator paper.

At the negative electrode we get **hydrogen**, which **burns** with a squeaky pop.

The solution left at the end contains **sodium hydroxide**.

21 Using the chemicals we make from salt

The three useful materials made by passing electricity through salt water are **chlorine**, **hydrogen** and sodium hydroxide.

Chlorine is used:
- in substances that kill **bacteria**
- to make a plastic called **PVC**
- to make **bleach**, which removes stains and fades colours.

Hydrogen is used:
- to make **ammonia**, which can be turned into fertiliser
- to change vegetable oils into **margarine**.

Paper and soap are both made using **sodium hydroxide**.

Hydrogen reacts with chlorine to make **hydrogen chloride**.

This dissolves in water to make hydrochloric **acid**.

22 The chemicals we use to make photographs

Silver chloride, silver bromide and silver iodide are all silver **halides**.

Light can change silver halides into **silver metal**. We say that light **reduces** silver halides to silver metal.

Silver halides are also reduced by **X-rays** and the radiation from **radioactive** substances.

We use silver halides to make photographic **film** and photographic paper.

Patterns of chemical change

1 Using heat to speed things up

Chemical reactions go at different speeds or **rates**.
Chemical reactions go faster at **higher** temperatures.
At low temperatures, chemical reactions **slow down**.

2 Making solutions react faster

When you dissolve a substance in water you get a **solution**.
A solution that contains a lot of dissolved substance is a **concentrated** solution. To make a concentrated solution react more slowly, you can **dilute** it.
To make gases react faster, you need a **high** pressure.

3 Making solids react faster

A solid can react with a liquid only where they touch. The reaction is on the **surface** of the solid.
If we break up the solid, we increase the total **surface area**. This means that smaller pieces react **faster**.

4 Substances that speed up reactions

A substance that speeds up a chemical reaction is called a **catalyst**.
The catalyst increases the rate of reaction but is not **used up**.
You can use catalysts **over** and **over** again.
Each chemical reaction needs its own **special** catalyst.
Useful materials such as margarine and sulphuric acid **cost** less to make when we use catalysts.

6 What makes chemical reactions happen?

For substances to react:
- their particles must **collide**;
- the particles must have enough **energy** when they do this.

The smallest amount of energy they need is called the **activation** energy.
If you increase the temperature, reactions happen faster. This is because the particles collide more **often** and with more **energy**.
Breaking solids into smaller pieces, making solutions more concentrated and increasing the pressure of gases all make reactions **faster**. All these things make the collisions between particles more **frequent**.

7 Getting energy out of chemicals

Charcoal, coal, gas and wood are all **fuels**.
When we **burn** them they release energy in the form of **heat**.
Many other chemical reactions also release **energy** into the surroundings. We call reactions like this **exothermic** reactions.

8 Do chemical reactions always release energy?

To make some chemical reactions happen you must **supply** energy.
We call these reactions **endothermic** reactions.
We must supply energy to extract metals from their ores.
We can supply this energy in the form of **heat** or **electricity**.
The chemical reactions in photography use **light** energy.

9 Living things can do our chemistry for us

We can use **living cells** to help us make new substances.
Examples of living things we can use in this way are **yeast** and **moulds**.
When we make wine and beer, we use yeast cells to turn **sugar** into **alcohol**. We call this reaction **fermentation**.
Yeast also makes the gas called **carbon dioxide**. The bubbles of this gas help bread to rise.

10 More cells that will work for us

The type of living cells that make yogurt are called **bacteria**.
They feed on the **sugar** in the milk and turn it into **lactic acid**.
To speed up their chemical reactions, living cells contain **enzymes**.
These need to be warm to work well, but must not get too hot as they are made from **protein**.
Protein **changes** when it is heated and cannot be changed back again.

11 Not too hot and not too cold

Food goes bad when **living cells** feed on it.
We can keep food fresh for longer by keeping it in a
fridge or a **freezer**. This is because living cells use
enzymes to speed up their reactions. These work
slowly if the temperature is **low**.
Useful living cells like yeast work best at temperatures
around **35 to 40°C**.

12 What use is nitrogen?

Plants need **nitrogen** for healthy growth.
About **78%** of the air is nitrogen but plants can't use
nitrogen gas directly. Instead, the plants take in
nitrates through their roots.
Farmers add nitrogen to the soil by using **fertilisers**.
This increases the **yield** of their crops.

13 Catching nitrogen to feed plants

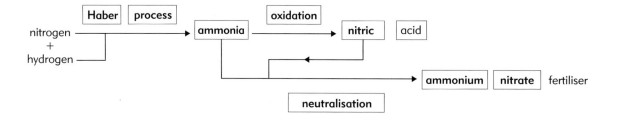

14 No chemicals, thank you

Fertilisers contain chemicals called **nitrates**. These
chemicals give plants the **nitrogen** that they need.
Nitrates can cause problems if they get into the **water**
supply because they are poisonous.
If nitrates get into rivers and lakes then they can
cause all of the living things to **die**.

15 How heavy are atoms?

Atoms are far too **small** to be easily weighed in
grams.
We compare the masses of atoms with each other.
This is called **relative** atomic mass or A_r for short.
The lightest element is **hydrogen**. It has an A_r
of **1 unit**.

16 Using relative atomic mass

To work out a relative molecular mass (M_r for short):
■ look up the relative **atomic** masses of the elements,
■ then **add** together the masses of all the atoms in the
  formula.

17 Elementary pie

Chemical compounds are made of **elements** (just as
an apple pie is made of ingredients).

19 Knowing when to be careful

Some substances have warning signs on them called
hazard symbols.
If a material catches fire easily it is **highly
flammable**.
If a material helps other substances to burn by
supplying oxygen, we say it is an **oxidising** substance.
We say that substances that can kill you are **toxic**.
Less dangerous substances are called **harmful**.
The skin can be destroyed or burned by **corrosive**
substances.
Substances that can redden the skin or make you
cough are **irritants**.

Glossary/index

[Notes Some words are used on lots of pages. Only the main ones are shown.]

A

A_r: short for *relative atomic mass*

acid, acidic: a solution that has a *pH* of less than 7; it will *neutralise* an *alkali*   20, 36–44

acid rain: rain with *nitrogen oxides* or *sulphur dioxide* dissolved in it, which make the rain acidic   86–87

alcohol: a substance produced by *fermentation*   151

alkali, alkaline: a solution that has a *pH* of more than 7; it will *neutralise* an *acid*   37–43, 45, 49

alkali metals: soft, reactive *metals* such as *potassium* and *sodium* in *Group* 1 of the *Periodic Table*; they react with *water* to produce *alkaline* solutions   45, 106–107, 118, 121

alloy: a mixture of *metals*   9, 11, 13

aluminium: a lightweight metal extracted from its ore by *electrolysis*   10, 23, 30–31

ammonia: a *gas* made from *hydrogen* and *nitrogen* by the *Haber process*   158

ammonium nitrate: a *fertiliser* made by *neutralising* nitric acid with *ammonia*   159

aqueous: dissolved in *water*   37

(aq): short for *aqueous*; used in *symbol equations*   20

atom: the smallest *particle* of an *element*   12, 102, 110–111, 120–123

B

basalt: an *extrusive igneous* rock containing small crystals   52–53, 60–61, 67

bauxite: *aluminium ore*; an *oxide*   30–31

blast furnace: used to extract *iron* from its *ore*   26–27, 149

boiling point: the temperature at which a *liquid* boils (when a *liquid* turns into a *gas*)   74–78, 101

brass: an *alloy of copper* and *zinc*   9

brittle: brittle materials break or crumble when you hit them; the opposite of *tough*   14

bromine: the only *non-metal element* that is a *liquid* at room temperature   15, 28

bronze: an *alloy* of *copper* and tin   9

burn: when a substance reacts with *oxygen* and releases heat   16–17, 82–89

C

calcium: a reactive *metal* found in *limestone*   18, 45

calcium carbonate: the chemical name for *limestone*

calcium hydroxide: the chemical name for *slaked lime*

calcium oxide: the chemical name for *quicklime*

carbon: a *non-metal element* found in the *molecules* of living things and *fossil fuels*   15, 23, 25, 76–81

carbon dioxide: a *gas* produced when substances containing *carbon burn*   26, 82–85, 88–89

carbon monoxide: a *toxic gas* produced when there isn't enough *oxygen* for *carbon* to *burn* completely   26, 85

catalysts: substances that increase the *rates* of chemical reactions   115, 140–141

cement: made from *limestone* and clay; used to make *concrete*   50

chlorides: *salts* made from *hydrochloric acid*   42

chlorine: a *toxic gas*; a *halogen* in *Group* 7 of the *Periodic Table*   28–29, 129–131

coke: a form of *carbon* used in a *blast furnace*   26

compound: a substance made from *atoms* of different *elements* joined together   24, 28

freeze, freezing: when a *liquid* changes to a *solid* by cooling   91

fuels: substances we *burn* to release energy   71, 78–79, 82–89, 146

G

gases: substances that spread out to fill all the space they can; one of the *states* of matter   92–93, 96–99

(g): short for *gas*; used in *symbol equations*

gneiss: a *metamorphic* rock   59, 60–61

gold: a rare, unreactive *metal* found as the metal itself in the Earth's *crust*   21, 24

granite: an *intrusive igneous* rock containing large crystals   53, 60–61

graphite: a form of *carbon* that is a *conductor* of electricity   6, 15

greenhouse gases: *gases* in the air that make the Earth warmer, for example *carbon dioxide*   88–89

Group: a family of similar *elements* in the same column of the *Periodic Table*   106–109, 112–121

H

Haber process: a process for making *ammonia* from *hydrogen* and *nitrogen*   158

halides: *compounds* of *metals* with *halogens*, for example *chlorides*   132–133

halogens: reactive *non-metal elements* such as *chlorine* and *bromine* in *Group* 7 of the *Periodic Table*   108–109, 119

hard materials: hard materials don't scratch or wear away easily   9

hazard symbols: hazard symbols tell you if substances are dangerous, for example *toxic* or *flammable* symbols   170–171

hydrocarbons: *compounds* containing the *elements* *hydrogen* and *carbon* only; *crude oil* is a mixture of hydrocarbons   76–83

hydrochloric acid: an *acid* that is produced by dissolving hydrogen chloride in water; this acid makes salts called chlorides   131

hydrogen: a *gas* that burns with a squeaky 'pop'; its *atoms* are the smallest of all   18, 20–21, 129–131

I

igneous rocks: rocks that form when molten *magma* or *lava* cools down   52–53, 60–61

indicators: substances with colours that depend on the *pH* of the solution they are in   38–39

intrusive rocks: *igneous* rocks that are formed inside the Earth's *crust*, for example *granite*   52–53, 60–61

ionic compounds: *compounds* made from *ions*   29, 123, 126–127

ions: *atoms* that have gained or lost *electrons* and so have a negative or positive electrical charge   16–17, 19–20, 22

iron: a common *metal*; *steel* contains mainly iron   16–17, 19–20, 22

isotopes: *atoms* of the same *element* that have different numbers of *neutrons* and so have different *mass numbers*   111

L

lava: *molten* rock from below the Earth's *crust* that has flowed out on to the surface   52

limestone: a common *sedimentary* rock with many uses; its chemical name is *calcium carbonate*   26–27, 46–48, 50–51, 55, 60–61

liquids: substances that have a definite volume but take the shape of the container in which you put them; one of the *states* of matter   90–91, 95

(l): short for *liquid*; used in *symbol equations*   20

M

M_r: short for *relative molecular mass*

magma: molten rock below the Earth's *crust*   52, 60, 62–63, 66–67, 69

magnesium: a reactive *metal*   16–18, 20, 22

mantle: the part of the Earth between the *crust* and the *core*   62

marble: a *metamorphic* rock formed from *limestone* 59, 60–61

mass number: the total number of *neutrons* and *protons* in the *nucleus* of an *atom* 110–111

melt, melting: when a *solid* changes to a *liquid* by heating 7, 91

melting point: the temperature at which a *solid* melts 7, 91

mercury: the only *element* that is a *liquid metal* at room temperature 7, 8

metals: *elements* that are *tough* and *conduct* electricity 6–8, 32–33

metamorphic rock: rock formed from another type of rock when it is heated and put under high pressure in the Earth's *crust* 58–59, 60–61

mixture: a mixture contains different substances that are not chemically joined together 9, 11, 13, 72, 74–75

molecular compound: a *compound* made from *atoms* of different *elements*, sharing *electrons* to form *molecules* 124–126

molecule: a molecule contains *atoms* that are joined together by sharing *electrons* 18, 76

molten substance: a substance that has been melted

N

neutral solution: a solution that is neither *acidic* nor *alkaline*; it has a *pH* of 7 37–39

neutralise, neutralisation: when an *acid* and an *alkali* react to make a *neutral* solution 40–43, 159

neutrons: *particles* in the *nucleus* of an *atom* that have no electrical charge; they have the same mass as *protons* 110–111

nitrates: *salts* produced from *nitric acid*; an important part of *fertilisers* 43, 156–161

nitric acid: an *acid* made by reacting *ammonia* with oxygen; this acid can be used to produce *salts* called *nitrates* 159

nitrogen: a not very reactive *gas* that makes up about $\frac{4}{5}$ of the air 26, 88, 156–159

nitrogen oxides: *compounds* of *nitrogen* and *oxygen* that cause *acid rain* 44, 87

noble gases: unreactive *gases* in *Group* 0 of the *Periodic Table* 112, 125

non-metals: *elements* that are not *metals* 14–15

nucleus: the central part of an *atom*, made of *protons* and *neutrons* 110

O

oil: see *crude oil*

ore: a *compound* from which a *metal* is extracted; often an *oxide* 24–27, 30–31, 34–35

oxides: *compounds* of *oxygen* and another *element* 16, 24, 30–31, 44–45

oxygen: a *gas* that makes up about $\frac{1}{5}$ of the air; it reacts with many other *elements* to form *oxides* 16–17

P

particles: the very small bits that scientists think everything is made of 94–102, 144–145

Periodic Table: a table of the *elements* that has similar elements placed in the same column or *Group* 12–13, 112–121

pH: a scale that tells you how *acidic* or *alkaline* a solution is 38–39

plastics: *compounds* made from *oil*; they are *polymers* 80–81

polymers: substances such as *plastics* made from very long *molecules* 81

potassium: a very reactive *alkali metal* 21, 45, 106–107

products: the substances that are made in chemical reactions 104

properties: what substances are like, for example reactive or unreactive, *brittle* or *tough* 6, 8, 80

proton number: the number of *protons* in an *atom* 110–111

protons: *particles* found in the *nucleus* of an *atom* that have a positive electrical charge; they have the same mass as *neutrons*   110–111

Q

quicklime: a substance made by heating *limestone*; its chemical name is *calcium oxide*   47–48

R

rate of reaction: how fast a reaction happens   134–143

reactants: the substances you start off with in a chemical reaction   104

reactivity series: a list of *elements* in order of how reactive they are   17–23

reduce, reduction: the process of obtaining a *metal* from its *ore*   25–26

relative atomic mass: the mass of an *atom* compared to other atoms   162–163

relative molecular mass: you get this by adding together the *relative atomic masses* of all the *atoms* in the *formula* of a *compound*   164–165

S

salt: 1. a *compound* you get when you *neutralise* an *acid* with an *alkali*   42–43, 109
    2. the everyday name for common salt or sodium chloride   128–131

sandstone: a *sedimentary* rock made from grains of sand   55, 60–61

schist: a *metamorphic* rock   59, 60–61

sediment: small bits of *solid* that settle at the bottom of a *liquid*   54–55

sedimentary rocks: rocks formed from layers of *sediment*   54–57, 60–61

silver halides: *compounds* of silver and a *halogen*   132–133, 149

slag: the *molten* waste produced in a *blast furnace*   27

slaked lime: a substance used to make soil less acidic; its chemical name is *calcium hydroxide*   48–49

slate: a *metamorphic* rock formed from mudstone   59, 60–61

sodium: a very reactive *alkali metal*   21, 45, 106–107

sodium hydroxide: a strong *alkali* that is used to make many other chemicals   131

solder: an *alloy* of tin and lead   13

solids: substances that keep their shape; one of the *states* of matter   90–91, 94

(s): short for *solid*; used in *symbol equations*   20

solution: a substance dissolved in *water*

stainless steel: an *alloy* of *steel* that does not rust   11

state: describes whether a substance is a *solid (s)*, a *liquid (l)*, a *gas (g)* or dissolved in water *(aq)*   93, 101

state symbol: a short way of writing the *state* of a substance   20, 105

steel: a cheap, strong, useful *metal* made mainly of *iron*   11, 16, 26–27

stiffness: stiff things don't bend easily   10

strength: strong materials don't break easily when you pull them or squeeze them   7

sulphates: *salts* made from sulphuric acid   43

sulphur: a yellow, *non-metal element*   14, 44

sulphur dioxide: a *gas* that causes *acid rain*   44, 86–87

symbol: a short way of writing an *element*, for example C = carbon   102

symbol equation: this shows the *reactants* and *products* in a chemical reaction using their *formulas*   20–21, 104–105

T

tectonic plates: very large pieces of the Earth's *crust*, which slowly move on the *molten magma* beneath them   64–69

toughness: a tough material doesn't break or crumble when you hit it; the opposite of *brittle*   7